STREET SPANISH 1

To order the accompanying cassette for

STREET SPANISH 1

See the coupon on the back page for details

STREET SPANISH 1

The Best of Spanish Slang

David Burke

John Wiley & Sons, Inc.

New York • Chichester • Weinheim • Brisbane • Singapore • Toronto

Design and Production: David Burke
Copy Editor: Alfonso Moreno-Santa
Front Cover Illustration: Ty Semaka
Inside Illustrations: Ty Semaka

Published by John Wiley & Sons, Inc.

Library of Congress Cataloging-in-Publication Data
Burke, David
Street Spanish 1 : the best of Spanish slang / David Burke.
p. cm.
ISBN 0-471-17970-1 (paper : alk. paper)
1. Spanish language—Slang. 2. Spanish language—Textbooks for foreign speakers—English. I. Title.
PC4961.B872 1997
468.2'421—dc21 97-21377
CIP

Printed in the United States of America
10 9 8 7 6 5 4 3

This book is dedicated to Debbie Wright:
my special friend, my adviser, my sister separated somewhere at birth.

ACKNOWLEDGMENTS

My special thanks to Alfonso Moreno-Santa for all his hard work and significant contribution to this book. His insight into the real Spanish language was indispensable. I feel extremely fortunate for having the opportunity to work with him and especially thankful for his wonderful friendship.

I'm forever grateful for finding Ty Semaka, a gifted illustrator who never ceases to amaze me with drawings that are infinitely clever, hilarious, and exciting.

I consider myself very fortunate to have been under the wing of so many wonderful people during the creation of this book. A tremendous and warm thanks goes to my pals at John Wiley & Sons: Gerry Helferich, Chris Jackson, Elaine O'Neal, Al Schwartz, and Benjamin Hamilton. They are without a doubt the most friendly, supportive, encouraging, and infinitely talented group of people with which I've had the pleasure to work.

Last but not least, a very special and heartfelt debt of gratitude goes to PJ Dempsey, my former editor at John Wiley & Sons. You're going to be a hard act to follow. You were the best. I miss you!

CONTENTS

INTRODUCTION

STREET SPANISH 1 has been updated with lots of new information to help you learn popular Spanish slang. This entertaining guide, geared for the student who has had three or more years of Spanish study, is a step-by-step approach to teaching the actual spoken language of the many Spanish-speaking countries that is constantly used in movies, books, and day-to-day business, as well as among family and friends. Now you can learn quickly the secret world of slang as you are introduced to the "inside" language that even a ten-year veteran of formalized Spanish would not understand!

STREET SPANISH 1 is designed to teach the essentials of Spanish slang in ten lessons, each divided into three primary parts:

- **DIALOGUE**

  In this section, popular slang words (understood universally throughout the Spanish-speaking countries) are presented in a dialogue on the left-hand page. A translation of the dialogue appears on the opposite page.

- **VOCABULARY**

  This section spotlights all of the slang terms that were used in the dialogue and offers:

  1. An example of usage for each entry;
  2. An English translation of the example;
  3. Synonyms, antonyms, variations, from various Spanish-speaking countries, and special notes to give you a complete sense of the word. For example:

pachanga *f.* party.

example:	Esta **pachanga** es muy divertida. Todo el mundo se lo está pasando muy bien.
translation:	This **party** is a lot of fun. Everybody is having a good time.
NOTE:	**ir de pachanga** *exp.* to go out and have a good time.
SYNONYM:	**parranda** *f.*

chismear *v.* to gossip.

example: A Pablo le encanta **chismear** sobre Anabel.

translation: Pablo loves to **gossip** about Anabel.

VARIATION: **chismorrear** *v.*

ALSO: **chisme** *m.* a juicy piece of gossip.

example: ¡Cuéntame los **chismes**!

translation: Give me the **dirt**!

- **PRACTICE THE VOCABULARY**

  These word games include all of the slang terms and idioms previously learned and will help you test yourself on your comprehension. This section includes fill-ins, crossword puzzles, word matches, find-a-word grids, multiple choice drills, and many more. *(The pages providing the answers to all the drills are indicated at the beginning of this section.)*

- **REVIEW**

  Following each sequence of five chapters is a summary review encompassing all the words and expressions learned up to that point.

The secret to learning **STREET SPANISH 1** is by following this simple checklist:

- Make sure that you have a good grasp on each section before proceeding to the drills. If you've made more than two errors in a particular drill, simply go back and review...then try again! *Remember:* This is a self-paced book, so take your time. You're not fighting the clock!
- It's very important that you feel comfortable with each chapter before proceeding to the next. Words learned along the way may crop up in the following dialogues. So feel comfortable before moving on!
- Make sure that you read the dialogues and drills aloud. This is an excellent way to become comfortable using these new terms and begin thinking like a native.

IMPORTANT: Slang must be used with discretion because it is an extremely casual "language" that certainly should not be practiced with formal dignitaries or employers that you are trying to impress! Most importantly, since a non-native speaker of Spanish may tend to sound forced or artificial using slang, your first goal should be to recognize and understand these types of words. Once you feel that you have a firm grasp on the usage of the slang words and expressions presented in this book, try using some in your conversations for extra color!

Just as a student of formalized English would be rather shocked to run into words like *pooped, zonked,* and *wiped out,* and discover that they all go under the heading of "tired," you too will be surprised and amused to encounter a whole new array of terms and phrases usually hidden away in the Spanish language and reserved only for the native speaker.

Welcome to the expressive and "colorful" world of Spanish slang!

Legend

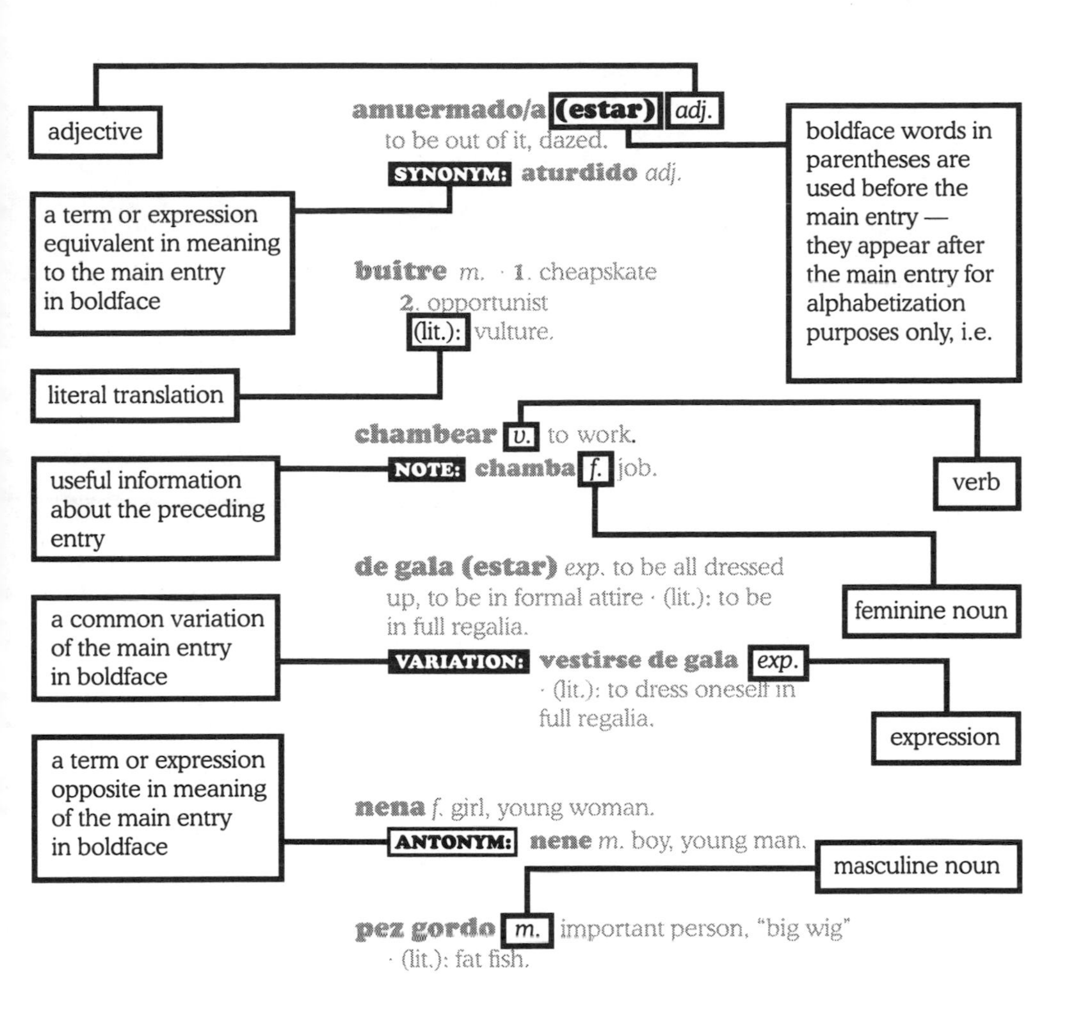

adjective
amuermado/a (estar) adj.
to be out of it, dazed.
SYNONYM: aturdido adj.
boldface words in parentheses are used before the main entry — they appear after the main entry for alphabetization purposes only, i.e.
a term or expression equivalent in meaning to the main entry in boldface
buitre m. · 1. cheapskate
2. opportunist
(lit.): vulture.
literal translation
chambear v. to work.
NOTE: chamba f. job.
useful information about the preceding entry
verb
de gala (estar) exp. to be all dressed up, to be in formal attire · (lit.): to be in full regalia.
feminine noun
a common variation of the main entry in boldface
VARIATION: vestirse de gala exp.
· (lit.): to dress oneself in full regalia.
expression
a term or expression opposite in meaning of the main entry in boldface
nena f. girl, young woman.
ANTONYM: nene m. boy, young man.
masculine noun
pez gordo m. important person, "big wig"
· (lit.): fat fish.

STREET SPANISH 1

LECCIÓN UNO

Hoy, *tropecé con* María en la calle.

(trans.): I ***bumped into*** *Maria in the street today.*
(lit.): I ***tripped with*** *Maria in the street today.*

Lección Uno

Dialogue in Slang

Hoy, tropecé con María en la calle.

Ana: Hoy, **tropecé** con María en la calle y me detuve a **platicar** con ella. ¡Siempre **se enrolla** mucho!

Inés: ¡**Caramba**! No soporto a esa **nena**. Deberías de haber intentado **evaporarte** en el **gentío**. Es que es tan **chocante**. Siempre está **chuleando**. Se cree que es mejor que nadie y en realidad es una a **donnadie**.

Ana: Ya sé. Todo lo que hizo esta vez fue **chismear** sobre Jorge, el **enano** de nuestra clase de biología. Yo le dije que no quería escucharla más, y que las únicas personas que hablan mal de otras a sus espaldas son **chusma**.

Inés: ¡Qué **guay**! Me alegro que le dijeras eso. Me **alucinas**. Nunca tienes miedo de decir lo que piensas.

Ana: Es que ella no sabe que yo soy **casinadie** y que ella es un **latón**.

Lesson One

Ana: Today I **bumped into** Maria in the street and stopped to **have a little chat** with her. She can really **talk up a storm**!

Inés: ¡**Geez**! I can't stand that **girl**. You should have tried to **disappear** in the **crowd**. Is she ever **annoying**. She's always trying to be so **cool**. She thinks she's better than everyone else and in reality she's the biggest **loser**.

Ana: I know. This time all she did was **gossip** about Jorge, the **short guy** in our biology class. I told her I didn't want to hear it and that people who talk badly about other people are nothing more than **scum**.

Inés: **Cool**! I'm glad you said that to her. You really **amaze** me. You're never afraid to say what's on your mind.

Ana: The thing is that she doesn't realize that I'm a **person with a lot of integrity** and she's a **pain in the neck**.

Vocabulary

alucinar *v.* to amaze, to astonish, to hallucinate.

example: Me **alucinaste** cuando te presentaste en la fiesta en bikini.

translation: You **astonished** me when you showed up at the party wearing a bikini.

SYNONYM -1: **eslembar** *v. (Puerto Rico / Cuba).*

SYNONYM -2: **flipar** *v. (Spain).*

caramba *interj.* geez, holy cow.

example: ¡**Caramba**!, no me puedo creer el calor que hace.

translation: **Geez**! I can't believe how warm it is.

SYNONYMS: SEE - **¡Hombre!**, *p. 72.*

casinadie *m.* a person of great integrity and influence, a very important person • (lit.): almost nobody.

example: ¡Mira! Por ahí viene el Señor Smith, es **casinadie** in esta compañía.

translation: Look! Here comes Mr. Smith. He's a **very important person** in this company.

ANTONYM: **donnadie** *m.* loser • (lit.): Mr. Nobody - SEE: *p. 5.*

chismear *v.* to gossip.

example: A Pablo le encanta **chismear** sobre Anabel.

translation: Pablo loves to **gossip** about Anabel.

VARIATION: **chismorrear** *v.*

ALSO: **chisme** *m.* a juicy piece of gossip.

example: ¡Cuéntame los **chismes**!

translation: Give me the **dirt**!

SYNONYM -1: **chusmear** *v. (Argentina).*

SYNONYM -2: **cotillear** *v. (Spain).*

chocante *adj.* annoying, unpleasant.

example: Ese tío habla demasiado, es muy **chocante**.

translation: That guy talks too much. He's really **annoying**.

NOTE: **chocar** *v.* to annoy, to get annoyed, to hate something or someone • (lit.): to crash, to collide.

example: Me **choca** ir de compras cuando hay mucha gente en las tiendas.

translation: I **hate** to go shopping when there are a lot of people in the stores.

chulear *v.* to act cool, to be vain or conceited, to show off.

example: Le encanta **chulear** de coche porque tiene un coche muy caro.

translation: He loves to **show off** his car because he drives an expensive car.

NOTE: **chulo/a** *adj.* cool, neat, good looking.

example: Ese hombre es muy **chulo**, siempre se viste con ropa cara.

translation: That guy is really **cool**. He always wears expensive clothes.

SYNONYM: **echándosear** *v. (Puerto Rico / Cuba).*

chusma *f.* despicable people, "scumbags."

example: Yo no voy a invitar a Jorge y Pedro a mi fiesta porque son **chusma**.

translation: I'm not inviting Jorge and Pedro to my party because they're **scum**.

donnadie *m.* loser • (lit.): Mr. Nobody.

example: Es tipo es un **donnadie**, no tiene dinero ni para pagar el alquiler.

translation: That guy is such a **loser**. He doesn't even have enough money to pay rent.

SYNONYM: **matada/o** *n. (Spain).*

ANTONYM: **casinadie** *m.* a very important person • (lit.): almost nobody - SEE: *p. 4*.

enano/a *n.* short person • (lit.): dwarf.

example: Mi maestro de literatura es tan **enano** que ni siquiera alcanza el pizarrón.

translation: My literature teacher is so **short** he can't even reach the blackboard.

SYNONYM: **hombrecito** *m. (Cuba).*

enrollarse *v.* **1.** to talk up a storm • **2.** to get involved romantically with someone • (lit.): to roll up, to wind.

example (1): A mi madre le gusta **enrollarse** mucho cuando viene visita a la casa.

translation: My mother loves to **talk up a storm** when she has company at her house.

example (2): Me encantaría **enrollarme** a esa tía porque es muy simpática y guapa.

translation: I'd love to **get involved** with that girl because she's very nice and beautiful.

SYNONYM: **cotorrear** *v. (Puerto Rico / Cuba)* • (lit.): to squawk (like a parrot).

NOTE: **charlatán/ana** *n.* blabbermouth.

evaporarse *v.* to disappear, to vanish • (lit.): to evaporate.

example: Me **evaporé** cuando me di cuenta que Juan estaba en la fiesta.

translation: I **disappeared** when I realized Juan was at the party.

SYNONYM -1: **colarse** *v. (Mexico)* • (lit.): to filter oneself.

SYNONYM -2: **escaquearse** *v. (Spain)* • (lit.): to check or checker oneself.

SYNONYM -3: **escurrirse** *v.* • (lit.): to slip, to slide, to sneak out.

SYNONYM -4: **esfumarse** *v.* • (lit.): to vanish.

gentío *m.* crowd, people.

example: No me gusta ir a los partidos de béisbol porque siempre hay mucho **gentío**.

translation: I don't like going to baseball games because there are always big **crowds** there.

SYNONYM: **gente** *f.* people, folks, relatives.

ALSO: **gente gorda** *f.* bigwigs • (lit.): fat people.

guay *adj.* cool, neat.

example: ¡Qué **guay**! ¡Esa motocicleta tiene tres ruedas!

translation: **Cool**! That motorcycle has three wheels!

SYNONYM -1: **chulo** *adj.*

SYNONYM -2: **padre** *adj.* • (lit.): father.

latón *n.* annoying person, pain in the neck.

example: Por favor, no invites a Maria a la fiesta mañana. ¡Es un **latón**!

translation: Please don't invite Maris to the party tonight. She's such a **pain in the neck**!

SYNONYM -1: **chinche** *m. (Puerto Rico / Cuba)* • (lit.): an annoying little bug.

SYNONYM -2: **dolor de cabeza (ser un)** *exp. (Cuba)* • (lit.): to be a pain in the head or headache.

SYNONYM -3: **lata** *f.* a pain in the neck • (lit.): tin can.

NOTE: Both *latón* and *lata* may be used when referring either to people or to things: *¡Qué lata!* or *¡Qué latón!* = What a pain in the neck!

SYNONYM -4: **latoso/a** *n. (Mexico).*

SYNONYM -5: **marrón** *m. (Spain).*

nena *f.* girl, young woman.

example: Creo que conozco a esa **nena**. La vi en en el centro comercial.

translation: I think I know that **girl**. I saw her at the mall.

SYNONYM -1: **mina** *f. (Argentina)* • (lit.): mine (as in "gold mine").

SYNONYM -2: **muchachita** *f. (Cuba).*

SYNONYM -3: **tía** *f. (Spain / Cuba)* • (lit.): aunt.

ANTONYM: **nene** *m.* boy, young man.

platicar *v. (Mexico)* to have a little chat, to talk.

example: Me encanta **platicar** con Darío. ¡Es tan inteligente y simpático!

translation: I love to **talk** with Darío. He's so smart and nice!

SYNONYM -1: **charlar** *v. (Argentina / Spain / Uruguay / Cuba).*

SYNONYM -2: **dar la lata** *exp. (Puerto Rico / Cuba).*

tropezar con alguien *exp.* to run into someone, to bump into someone • (lit.): to trip or stumble with someone.

example: Ayer **tropecé con** Antonio Rodriquez y lo encontré muy delgado.

translation: Yesterday I **bumped into** Antonio Rodriquez and he looked really thin to me.

SYNONYM -1: **chocarme con alguien** *exp. (Argentina)* • (lit.): to collide oneself with someone.

SYNONYM -2: **toparse con alguien** *exp. (Spain / Puerto Rico / Cuba)* • (lit.): to bump oneself with someone.

Practice the Vocabulary 

(Answers to Lesson 1, p. 171)

A. Underline the appropriate word(s) that best complete(s) the phrase.

1. No te imaginas con quien me (**calabacé**, **tropecé**, **traje por los pelos**) en el mercado hoy.
2. Inés habla mucho. Siempre se (**rasca**, **reposa**, **enrolla**) mucho.
3. Me encanta (**platicar**, **presumir**, **practicar**) con Alfredo. Es muy interesante.
4. ¡(**Caramba**, **Carambola**, **Cachis**)! ¡Qué frío hace!
5. Manuel es tan (**chocante**, **chocador**, **cantante**) que nadie quiere ser su amigo.
6. Ese tipo es un (**señornadie**, **donnadie**, **nadie**). No tiene dinero ni para ir al cine.
7. No me gusta ese barrio porque está lleno de (**chamba**, **chispas**, **chusma**).
8. Esa (**nena**, **nenuca**, **nana**) es muy guapa.
9. No soporto a Jorge. ¡Es un (**latero**, **latucho**, **latón**)!
10. ¡Qué (**guay**, **gato**, **guinda**)! Ese automóvil es precioso.
11. Cuando vi a Luis quería (**evaporarme**, **escoltarme**, **encantarme**) porque no quería hablar con él.
12. Mi maestro de historia es tan (**eléboro**, **enano**, **elegido**) que no alcanza el pizarrón.

B. Complete the following phrases by choosing the appropriate word(s) from the list below. Make all necessary changes.

alucinar	**chusma**	**guay**
chismear	**donnadie**	**latón**
chocante	**evaporarse**	**platicar**
chulear	**gentío**	**tropezar con**

1. Ese tipo es un ________________ . No tiene dinero ni para cenar.

2. Cuando vi a Juan quería ________________ porque no quería que me viera.

3. Ayer ________________ Luis y me dijo que acababa de conseguir un trabajo nuevo.

4. Ayer había un gran ________________ en el gran almacén.

5. Me ________________ cuando te presentaste en la escuela en ese vestido tan atrevido.

6. No me gusta esa discoteca porque está llena de ________________ .

7. A Luis le encanta ________________ sobre Angélica.

8. No me gusta Pedro porque es un ________________ .

9. ¡Qué ________________! Pedro acaba de comprarse una motocicleta nueva.

10. A Lola le encanta ________________ . Nunca cierra la boca.

11. A Adolfo le encanta ________________ de motocicleta porque tiene una Harley-Davidson.

12. Andrés habla demasiado. Es un ________________ .

C. Match the Spanish phrases with the English translations by writing the appropriate letter in the box.

☐ 1. Mateo loves to gossip about David.

☐ 2. He loves to show off his house.

☐ 3. Gee! I can't believe how cold it is.

☐ 4. Cool! What a nice house you have!

☐ 5. I love to talk to Enrique.

☐ 6. I think I've seen that girl before.

☐ 7. I disappeared when I saw him there.

☐ 8. That guy is such a loser.

☐ 9. My wife loves to talk up a storm.

☐ 10. Yesterday I bumped into Pedro.

☐ 11. Rosa is such a pain in the neck!

☐ 12. All of José's friends are scum.

A. **¡Caramba!, no me puedo creer el frío que hace.**

B. **¡Qué guay! ¡Qué casa más bonita tienes!**

C. **Me encanta platicar con Enrique.**

D. **Creo que he visto a esa nena antes.**

E. **Le encanta chulear de casa.**

F. **Ese tipo es un donnadie.**

G. **Me evaporé cuando le vi allí.**

H. **A mi esposa le encanta enrollarse mucho.**

I. **Todos los amigos de José son chusma.**

J. **Rosa es un verdadero latón.**

K. **Ayer tropecé con Pedro.**

L. **A Mateo le encanta chismear sobre David.**

D. CROSSWORD

Fill in the crossword puzzle on page 15 by choosing the correct word(s) from the list below.

alucinar	**chusma**	**guay**
caramba	**donnadie**	**latón**
casinadie	**enano**	**nena**
chismear	**enrollarse**	**platicar**
chocante	**evaporarse**	**tropezar**
chulear	**gentío**	

ACROSS

14. example: Por favor, no invites a María a la fiesta. ¡Es un ______!

translation: Please don't invite Maria to the party. She's such a **pain in the neck**!

16. example: ¡Qué ______! ¡Esa motocicleta tiene tres ruedas!

translation: **Cool**! That motorcycle has three wheels!

24. example: Yo no voy a invitar a Jorge y Pedro a mi fiesta porque son ______.

translation: I'm not inviting Jorge and Pedro to my party because they're **scum**.

29. example: No quiero ______ con David porque es un pesado.

translation: I don't want to **run into** David because he's such a pain in the neck.

37. example: ¡______!, no me puedo creer el calor que hace.

translation: **Geez**! I can't believe how warm it is.

44. example: Mi maestro de literatura es tan ______ que ni siquiera alcanza el pizarrón.

translation: My literature teacher is so **short** he can't even reach the blackboard.

51. example: Es tipo es un ______, no tiene dinero ni para pagar el alquiler.

translation: That guy is such a **loser**. He doesn't even have enough money to pay rent.

58. example: A mi madre le gusta ______ mucho cuando viene visita a la casa.

translation: My mother loves to **talk up a storm** when she has company at her house.

DOWN

5. example: Me encanta ______ con Darío, ¡es tan inteligente!

translation: I love to **talk** with Dario. He's so smart!

12. example: Ese tío habla demasiado, es muy ______.

translation: That guy talks too much. He's really **annoying**.

16. example: No me gusta ir a los partidos de béisbol porque siempre hay mucho ______.

translation: I don't like going to baseball games because there are always big **crowds** there.

24. example: Le encanta ______ de coche porque tiene un coche muy caro.

translation: He loves to **show off** his car because he drives a Mercedez-Benz.

30. example: Quería ______ cuando me di cuenta que Juan estaba en la fiesta.

translation: I wanted to **disappear** when I realized Juan was at the party.

36. example: ¡Mira! Por ahí viene el Sr. Smith, es ______ en esta compañía.

translation: Look! Here comes Mr. Smith. He's a **very important person** in this company.

38. example: Voy a ______ si te presentas en la fiesta en bikini.

translation: I'm going to be **astonished** if you show up at the party wearing a bikini.

40. example: A Pablo le encanta ______ sobre Anabel.

translation: Pablo loves to **gossip** about Anabel.

52. example: Creo que conozco a esa ______, la vi en en el centro comercial.

translation: I think I know that **girl**. I saw her at the mall.

CROSSWORD PUZZLE

E. DICTATION
Test Your Aural Comprehension

(This dictation can be found in the Appendix on page 189.)

If you are following along with your cassette, you will now hear a series of sentences from the opening dialogue. These sentences will be read by a native speaker at normal conversational speed (which may seem fast to you at first). In addition, the words will be pronounced *as you would actually hear them in a conversation,* oftentimes including some common reductions.

The first time the sentences are presented, simply listen in order to get accustomed to the speed and heavy use of reductions. The sentences will then be read again with a pause after each to give you time to write down what you heard. The third time the sentences are read, follow along with what you have written.

LECCIÓN DOS

¡Yo creo que Juan se ha *chupado* demasiadas *chelas*!

(trans.): I think Juan **drank** a few too many **beers**!
(lit.): I think Juan **sucked** a few too many **beers**!

Lección Dos

Dialogue in Slang

¡Yo creo que Juan se ha chupado demasiadas chelas!

Ricardo: Mira quien acaba de **colarse** en el bar…Teresa Lopez. Oye, esta noche está **de gala**. ¡Es una verdadera **buenona**!

Adriana: Estoy segura de que le gustaría el **piropo**. Dime, ¿Conoces a ese **tío** con el **pitillo** en la **bocaza**?

Ricardo: ¿Te refieres al **gafudo** que está al lado de la **foca**? Nunca le había visto antes.

Adriana: Es Juan Valdez. Me sorprende verlo en esta **pachanga**. Solía ser un **empollón** pero de repente se ha convertido en un **cachas**. ¡Qué **jeta**! ¡Y además está **cuadrado**!

Ricardo: Yo creo que se ha **chupado** demasiadas **chelas**. Me parece que está **bebido**. ¡No me sorprendería nada si se levanta mañana con una **cruda**!

Lesson Two

Ricardo: Look who just **cut in line** at the bar...Teresa Lopez. She looks **beautiful** tonight. She's a real **knockout**!

Adriana: I'm sure she'd appreciate the **compliment**. Say, do you know that **guy** with the **cigarette** hanging from his **mouth**?

Ricardo: Are you referring to the **guy wearing glasses** next to the **fat lady**? I've never seen him before.

Adriana: That's Juan Valdez. I'm surprised to see him at this **party**. He used to be the biggest **nerd** but suddenly turned into a real **hunk**. What a **face**! And he's so **strong**, too!

Ricardo: I also think he **drank** a few too many **beers**. He looks kind of **wasted** to me. I wouldn't be surprised if he wakes up with a real **hangover** tomorrow morning!

Vocabulary

bebido/a (estar) *adj.* to be drunk, "wasted," inebriated.

example: Creo que Pedro está **bebido** porque no se puede mantener en pie.

translation: I think Pedro is **wasted** because he can't even stand up.

SYNONYM -1: **alegre (estar)** *adj.* • (lit.): to be happy.

SYNONYM -2: **borrachín (estar)** *adj.*

NOTE: This comes from the adjective *borracho/a* meaning "drunk."

SYNONYM -3: **cuba (estar)** *adj.*

SYNONYM -4: **en pedo** *adj. (Argentina)* • (lit.): in fart.

SYNONYM -5: **pellejo (estar)** *adj.* • (lit.): to be skin (as in chicken skin).

SYNONYM -6: **piripi (estar)** *adj.*

SYNONYM -7: **tomado/a (estar)** *adj.* • (lit.): to be drunk/taken.

bocaza *f.* mouth, big mouth.

example: ¡Ese tipo tiene la **bocaza** tan grande como la de un tiburón!

translation: That guy's **mouth** is as big as a shark's!

SYNONYM: **bocacha** *f.*

buenona *f.* beautiful woman, a knockout.

example: La profesora nueva de matemáticas es una verdadera **buenona**.

translation: The new math teacher is a real **knockout**.

SYNONYM -1: **buenachón** *f. (Puerto Rico).*

SYNONYM -2: **cuero** *m.* • (lit.): skin.

SYNONYM -3: **diosa** *f. (Argentina)* • (lit.): goddess.

SYNONYM -4: **potra** *f. (Argentina).*

SYNONYM -5: **tía buena** *f. (Spain / Cuba)* • (lit.): aunt good.

cachas *m.* good-looking young man, a hunk.

example: Sergio está haciendo mucho deporte últimamente. Se está convirtiendo en un **cachas**.

translation: Sergio is doing a lot of exercise lately. He's becoming a real **hunk**.

SYNONYM -1: **canchero** *m. (Argentina)* • (lit.): expert, skilled.

SYNONYM -2: **langa** *m. (Argentina).*

NOTE: This is a reverse transformation of the word *galán* (lan-ga) meaning "gallant" or "handsome."

SYNONYM -3: **tío bueno** *m. (Cuba / Spain)* • (lit.): uncle good.

SYNONYM -4: **tofete** *m. (Puerto Rico).*

SYNONYM -5: **tremendo tipazo** *m. (Cuba).*

chela *f.* beer • (lit.): blond.

example: En ese restaurante sirven **chelas** de México.

translation: They serve Mexican **beer** in that restaurant.

SYNONYM -1: **birra** *f. (Argentina).*

SYNONYM -2: **palo** *m. (Puerto Rico)* beer or any strong drink • (lit.): stick (since when one gets drunk, it could be compared to being hit on the head with a stick, causing dizziness and fogginess).

chupar *v.* to drink • (lit.): to suck, to absorb.

example: A Manolo le gusta **chupar** demasiado.

translation: Manolo likes to **drink** too much.

SYNONYM -1: **darle al chupe** *exp.* to drink • (lit.): to take the pacifier (baby's comforter).

SYNONYM -2: **dar palos** *exp. (Puerto Rico)* • (lit.): to give (oneself) sticks (which is a slang synonym for "drinks" since when one gets drunk, it could be compared to being hit on the head with a stick, causing dizziness and fogginess).

colarse *v.* to cut in line.

example: Me fastidia cuando la gente intenta **colarse** en frente de mí.

translation: I hate it when people try to **cut in line** in front of me.

cruda *f.* hangover • (lit.): raw.

example: Si bebes mucho hoy, mañana tendrás una **cruda**.

translation: If you drink a lot today, you'll have a **hangover** tomorrow.

SYNONYM -1: **goma (estar de)** *exp.* to be like rubber.

SYNONYM -2: **resaca** *f.* • (lit.): undertow.

cuadrado/a (estar) *adj.* (pronounced *cuadrao* in Cuba and Puerto Rico) to be strong, muscular • (lit.): to be squared.

example: Ricardo está **cuadrado**, se nota que hace ejercicio.

translation: Ricardo is so **strong**, you can tell he exercises.

SYNONYM: **mula (estar como una)** *exp.* • (lit.): to be like a mule.

de gala (estar) *exp.* to be all dressed up, to be in formal attire, to be dressed to kill • (lit.): to be in full regalia.

example: Siempre que voy a una fiesta me visto **de gala**.

translation: I always get **all dressed up** when I go to a party.

VARIATION: **vestirse de gala** *exp.* • (lit.): to dress oneself in full regalia.

empollón/na *n.* nerd, geek, pain in the neck.

example: Francisco siempre está estudiando. Es un verdadero **empollón**.

translation: Francisco is always studying. He's a real **nerd**.

NOTE: **empollar** *v.* to study hard • (lit.): to hatch, brood.

SYNONYMS: SEE - **adoquín**, *p. 68.*

foca *f.* a very fat woman • (lit.): seal.

example: Adriana es una **foca**. Parece que siempre está comiendo.

translation: Adriana is really **fat**. It seems like she's always eating.

SYNONYM -1: **elefante** *m.* • (lit.): elephant.

SYNONYM -2: **gordita** *f. (Cuba).*

SYNONYM -3: **vaca** *f. (Puerto Rico* • (lit.): cow.

gafudo/a • **1.** *adj.* said of one who wears glasses, "four-eyed" • **2.** *n.* one who wears glasses, "four-eyes."

example (1): El policía **gafudo** me dio una multa.

translation: That **four-eyed** policeman gave me a ticket.

example (2): Ese **gafudo** es mi nuevo profesor de biología.

translation: That **four-eyed man** is my new biology teacher.

SYNONYM -1: **anteojudo** *m. (Argentina).*

SYNONYM -2: **cuatroojos** *m.* • (lit.): four-eyes.

SYNONYM -3: **gafas** *f.pl. (Cuba)* • (lit.): glasses.

SYNONYM -4: **gafitas** *adj. & n.* • (lit.): small pair of glasses.

jeta *f.* face.

example: ¡Qué **jeta**! ¡Marisa es guapísima!

translation: What a **face**! Marisa is beautiful!

ALSO: ¡Qué **jeta**! *exp.* What nerve!

pachanga *f.* party.

example: Esta **pachanga** es muy divertida. Todo el mundo se lo está pasando muy bien.

translation: This **party** is a lot of fun. Everybody is having a good time.

NOTE: **ir de pachanga** *exp.* to go out and have a good time.

SYNONYM -1: **boliche** *f. (Argentina).*

SYNONYM -2: **fiestón** *m. (Puerto Rico)*

SYNONYM -3: **movida** *f. (Spain).*

SYNONYM -4: **parranda** *f.*

SYNONYM -5: **reventón** *m.* • (lit.): bursting, explosion.

piropo *m.* compliment.

example: A Ana siempre le echan muchos **piropos** porque es una mujer muy bella.

translation: Ana always receives many **compliments** because she's a very beautiful woman.

NOTE: **echar un piropo** *exp.* to give a compliment.

pitillo *m.* cigarette • (lit.): small whistle.

example: Pedro tiene mal aliento porque siempre tiene un **pitillo** en la boca.

translation: Pedro has bad breath because he always has a **cigarette** hanging from his mouth.

SYNONYM -1: **faso** *m. (Argentina).*

SYNONYM -2: **pucho** *m. (Argentina)* • (lit.): cigarette butt.

tío *m. (Cuba / Spain)* guy, "dude" • (lit.): uncle.

example: Conozco a ese **tío**. Solía ir a mi escuela.

translation: I know that **guy**. He used to go to my school.

NOTE: **tía** *f.* girl, "chick" • (lit.): aunt.

SYNONYM: **tipo** *m. (Mexico / Puerto Rico / Argentina)* guy, "dude" • (lit.): type.

ALSO: **tipa** *f.* girl, "chick" • (lit.): type.

Practice the Vocabulary 

(*Answers to Lesson 2, p. 172*)

A. Rewrite the following sentences by replacing the italicized word(s) with the slang synonym from the right column.

1. Parece que Jorge está *borracho*.

   ____

2. Ese tipo está *muy musculoso*.

   ____

3. Pedro tiene la *boca* muy grande.

   ____

4. Esa mujer está *muy bonita*.

   ____

5. Quiero ir a la *fiesta* de Juan.

   ____

A. **cuadrado**

B. **cachas**

C. **gafudo**

D. **foca**

E. **de gala**

6. Ese hombre *usa gafas*.

    ____

7. Javier es muy *estudioso*.

    ____

8. Marta es *muy gorda*.

    ____

9. Marisol está *muy elegante* esta noche.

    ____

10. Antonio fuma demasiados *cigarrillos*.

    ____

11. A Marco le gusta *beber* demasiado.

    ____

12. Ese tipo es *muy guapo*.

    ____

F. **pachanga**

G. **bocaza**

H. **empollón**

I. **buenona**

J. **bebido**

K. **pitillos**

L. **chupar**

B. Complete the following phrases by choosing the appropriate word(s) from the list below. Make any necessary changes.

chelas	**colarse**	**gafudo**
bocaza	**cruda**	**jeta**
buenona	**empollón**	**piropo**
cachas	**foca**	**tío**

1. Ayer bebí demasiado. Hoy tengo una ________________.

2. Andrea es una mujer muy bonita. Es una verdadera ____________.

3. Esos niños intentaron ________________ en el cine.

4. Ese ________________ no ve nada.

5. Para mi gusto las ________________ de Alemania son las mejores.

6. ¡Qué ________________! Pedro no tiene vergüenza de nada.

7. Ese tipo tiene una ________________ muy grande.

8. ¡Conozco a ese ________________! Solía ser mi vecino.

9. David es muy guapo. Todas las mujeres piensan que es un _______.

10. María come tanto que se ha convertido en una verdadera _______.

11. Juan es un ________________. Siempre está estudiando.

12. Siempre que Ana pasa por una construcción recibe muchos ________________.

C. Underline the synonym.

1. **bocaza**:
   a. boca
   b. bocado

2. **cachas**:
   a. hombre feo
   b. hombre guapo

3. **cruda**:
   a. dolor de muelas
   b. dolor de cabeza

4. **pachanga**:
   a. fierro
   b. fiesta

5. **jeta**:
   a. cara
   b. nariz

6. **pitillo**:
   a. silbato
   b. cigarrillo

7. **gafudo**:
   a. persona con gafas
   b. persona con la nariz muy grande

8. **foca**:
   a. mujer muy gorda
   b. mujer muy delgada

9. **estar de gala**:
   a. estar elegante
   b. estar vestido para hacer ejercicio

10. **chupar**:
    a. comer
    b. beber o tomar

11. **buenona**:
    a. mujer fea
    b. mujer guapa

12. **chela**:
    a. cerveza
    b. vino

D. Complete the dialogue using the list below.

bebido	**colarse**	**gafudo**
bocaza	**cruda**	**jeta**
buenona	**cuadrado**	**pachanga**
cachas	**de gala**	**piropo**
chelas	**empollón**	**pitillo**
chupado	**foca**	**tío**

Ricardo: Mira quien acaba de ____________ en el bar...Teresa Lopez. Oye, esta noche está ____________ . ¡Es una verdadera ____________!

Adriana: Estoy segura de que le gustaría el ____________ . Dime, ¿Conoces a ese ____________ con el ____________ en la ____________?

Ricardo: ¿Te refieres al ____________ que está al lado de la ____________? Nunca le había visto antes.

Adriana: Es Juan Valdez. Me sorprende verlo en esta ______________ .
Solía ser un ______________ pero de repente se ha convertido
en un ______________ . ¡Qué ______________! ¡Y además
está ______________!

Ricardo: Yo creo que se ha ______________ demasiadas ___________ .
Me parece que está ______________ . ¡No me sorprendería
nada si se levanta mañana con una ______________!

E. WORD SEARCH
Using the list below, circle the words in the sphere on page 32 that fit the following expressions. Words may be spelled up, down, or across.

bebido	**chupar**	**gafudo**
bocaza	**cruda**	**jeta**
buenona	**cuadrado**	**pachanga**
cachas	**foca**	**pitillo**

1. example: La profesora de matemáticas es una verdadera ______.
   translation: The math teacher is a real **knockout**.

2. example: Pedro tiene mal aliento porque siempre tiene un ______ en la boca.
   translation: Pedro has bad breath because he always has a **cigarette** hanging from his mouth.

3. example: Si bebes hoy, mañana tendrás una ______.
   translation: If you drink today, you'll have a **hangover** tomorrow.

4. example: Ricardo está ______, se nota que hace ejercicio.

   translation: Ricardo is so **strong**, you can tell he exercises.

5. example: Sergio ha hecho mucho deporte últimamente. Se está convirtiendo en un ______.

   translation: Sergio is doing a lot of exercise lately. He's becoming a real **hunk**.

6. example: El policía ______ me dio una multa.

   translation: That **four-eyed** policeman gave me a ticket.

7. example: ¡Qué ______! ¡Marisa es guapísima!

   translation: What a face! Marisa is **beautiful**!

8. example: Creo que Pedro está ______ porque no se puede mantener en pie.

   translation: I think Pedro's **wasted** because he can't even stand up.

9. example: Adriana es una ______. Parece que siempre está comiendo.

   translation: Adriana is really **fat**. It seems like she's always eating.

10. example: ¡Ese tipo tiene la ______ tan grande como la de un tiburón!

    translation: That guy's **mouth** is as big as a shark's!

11. example: A Manolo le gusta ______ demasiado.

    translation: Manolo likes to **drink** too much.

12. example: Esta ______ es muy divertida. Todo el mundo se lo está pasando muy bien.

    translation: This **party**'s a lot of fun. Everyone's having a good time.

FIND-A-WORD SPHERE

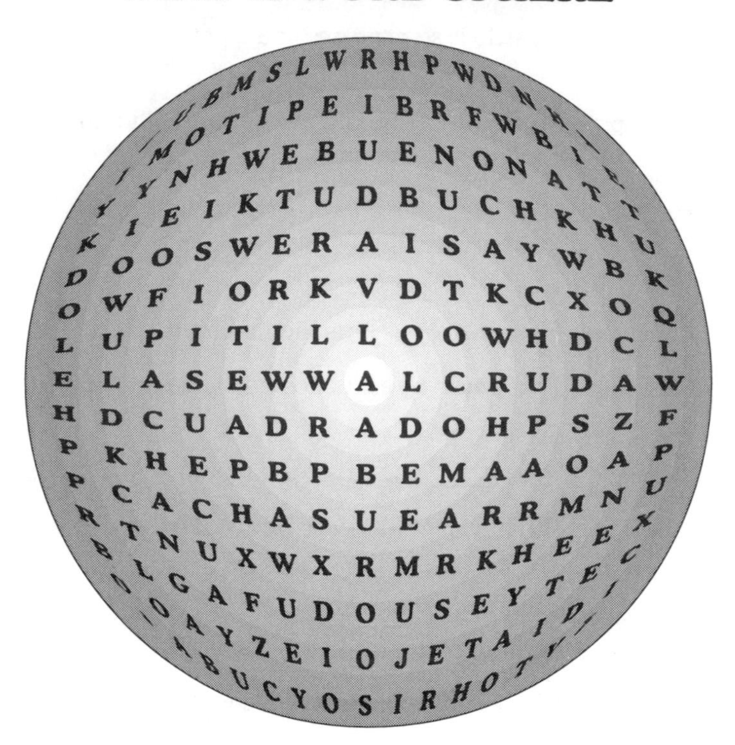

F. DICTATION
Test Your Aural Comprehension

(This dictation can be found in the Appendix on page 189.)

If you are following along with your cassette, you will now hear a series of sentences from the opening dialogue. These sentences will be read by a native speaker at normal conversational speed (which may seem fast to you at first). In addition, the words will be pronounced *as you would actually hear them in a conversation,* oftentimes including some common reductions.

The first time the sentences are presented, simply listen in order to get accustomed to the speed and heavy use of reductions. The sentences will then be read again with a pause after each to give you time to write down what you heard. The third time the sentences are read, follow along with what you have written.

LECCIÓN TRES

Alfonso es un *pez gordo* en su compañía.

(trans.): Alfonso is a ***big wig*** *in his company.*
(lit.): Alfonso is a ***fat fish*** *in his company.*

Lección Tres

Dialogue in Slang

Alfonso es un pez gordo en su compañía.

Tomás: ¡Estoy **en ascuas**! ¿Qué pasó?

David: Bueno, no quiero que pienses que soy un **cuentista**, pero el jefe acusó a Ricardo de **mangar** de la compañía. Y cuando el **pez gordo** lo averiguó, hasta llamó a la **poli**. Yo no me puedo creer que Ricardo es un **mangante**. Ha **currado** aquí dos años, gana mucha **lana** y siempre me ha parecido un **chico** muy decente.

Tomás: **A que** el jefe estaba **trastornado** cuando se dio cuenta. ¡Qué **gazpacho**! ¿Por qué haría Ricardo una **chorrada** como esa y arriesgarse a perder su **enchufe**?, o lo que es peor, acabar en el **talego**. ¡Qué **besugo**! Ya estaba **fichado** por el jefe, pero ¡esto es **el colmo**!

Lesson Three

Tomás: I'm **on pins and needles**! What happened?

David: Well, I don't want you to think that I'm a **gossip**, but the boss accused Ricardo of **stealing** from the company. And when the **big cheese** found out, he even called the **cops**. I have trouble believing that Ricardo is a **thief**. He's **worked** here for two years, makes **big bucks** and always seemed like a very honest **guy**.

Tomás: **I bet** the boss was **furious** when he found out. What a **mess**! Why would Ricardo do such a **stupid thing** like that and risk losing his **job**? Or worse, end up in **jail**? What an **idiot**! He was already on the boss's **bad side** but this **takes the cake**!

Vocabulary

a que *exp.* I'll bet (you) • (lit.): to that.

example: **A que** llueve el día de mi cumpleaños.

translation: **I'll bet you** it rains on my birthday.

ascuas (estar en) *exp.* to be on pins and needles.

example: Estoy **en ascuas**. ¡No sé si voy a pasar el examen de matemáticas!

translation: I'm **on pins and needles**. I don't know if I'm going to pass the math test!

SYNONYM -1: **bolas (estar en)** *exp. (Argentina)* • (lit.): to be in balls (perhaps since one's hands may be clenched during times of great anticipation).

SYNONYM -2: **loco/a por saber algo (estar)** *exp. (Cuba)* • (lit.): to be crazy to know something.

besugo *m.* idiot, fool, harebrained person, scatterbrain • (lit.): sea bream (which is a kind of fish).

example: Jorge es un **besugo**. Siempre comete errores.

translation: Jorge is an **idiot**. He's always making mistakes.

SYNONYMS: SEE - **adoquín**, *p. 68.*

cuentista *m.&f.* gossip • (lit.): story teller.

example: Sergio siempre está hablando de otras personas. ¡Es un **cuentista**!

translation: Sergio is always talking about other people. He's such a **gossip**!

SYNONYM -1: **cantamañanas** *m.*

SYNONYM -2: **chismoso** *m. (Argentina).*

SYNONYM -3: **mitotero/a** *n. (Mexico).*

chico *m.* boy, guy, "dude."

example: Ese **chico** siempre se viste bien.

translation: That **guy** always dresses well.

NOTE: **chica** *f.* girl, "chick."

SYNONYM -1: **chamaco/a** *n. (Mexico / Puerto Rico).*

SYNONYM -2: **guambito** *m. (Columbia).*

SYNONYM -3: **nene** *m. (Argentina / Uruguay / Spain) guy* • **nena** *f.* girl.

SYNONYM -4: **patojo/a** *n. (Guatemala).*

SYNONYM -5: **pibe** *n. (Argentina / Uruguay / Spain).*

SYNONYM -6: **tío** *m. (Cuba / Spain)* • (lit.): uncle.

chorrada *f.* stupid or despicable act.

example: No me puedo creer que Pablo hizo una **chorrada** como esa.

translation: I can't believe Pablo would do a **stupid thing** like that.

NOTE: The noun *chorrada* may also be used when referring to something very easy to do.

SYNONYM -1: **burrada** *f. (Mexico)* a stupid act or remark • (lit.): a drove of donkeys • *decir burradas;* to talk nonsense.

SYNONYM -2: **porquería** *f. (Cuba)* • (lit.): filth.

SYNONYM -3: **trastada** *f. (Puerto Rico).* despicable act or dirty trick.

colmo (ser el) *exp.* to take the cake, to be the last straw • (lit.): to be the culmination.

example: David no ha pagado el alquiler en tres meses. ¡Esto **es el colmo**!

translation: David hasn't paid the rent for three months. That **takes the cake**!

VARIATION: **colmo de los colmos (ser el)** *exp.* • (lit.): to be the culmination of culminations.

currar *v.* to work.

example: Me encanta **currar** en este restaurante porque así nunca tengo hambre.

translation: I love **working** at this restaurant because that way I never go hungry.

SYNONYM -1: **afanar** *v. (Argentina).*

SYNONYM -2: **chambear** *v.*

NOTE: **chamba** *m.* job.

enchufe *m.* cushy job • (lit.): plug, socket.

example: Manuel consiguió un buen trabajo porque tiene un buen **enchufe**.

translation: Manuel got a **cushy job** because he has good connections.

ALSO: **tener enchufe** *exp.* to have connections.

SYNONYM -1: **chollo** *m.*

SYNONYM -2: **laburo** *m. (Argentina).*

SYNONYM -3: **momio** *m.* • (lit.): that which is lean.

SYNONYM -4: **pala** *f. (Puerto Rico)* • (lit.): shovel.

fichado/a (estar) *adj.* to be on someone's bad side, to be on someone's bad list • (lit.): to be posted or affixed.

example: Creo que el maestro tiene **fichado** a Pepe porque siempre le está gritando.

translation: I think Pepe's on the teacher's **bad side** because he's always yelling at him.

VARIATION: **fichado/a (tener)** *exp.* • (lit.): to have posted or affixed.

SYNONYM -1: **cazar alguien** *v. (Cuba)* • (lit.): to hunt someone down.

SYNONYM -2: **tener en la mirilla** *exp.* • (lit.): to have someone on target.

gazpacho *m. (Spain)* mess, predicament, jam • (lit.): a type of Spanish tomato soup.

example: El tráfico de Los Angeles es un verdadero **gazpacho**.

translation: Los Angeles traffic is a real **mess**.

SYNONYM -1: **broncón** *m. (Mexico).*

SYNONYM -2: **caos** *m.* • (lit.): chaos.

SYNONYM -3: **desbarajuste** *m.* • (lit.): disorder, confusion.

SYNONYM -4: **despelote** *m.*

SYNONYM -5: **embole** *m. (Argentina).*

SYNONYM -6: **embrollo** *m.* • (lit.): muddle, tangle, confusion.

SYNONYM -7: **enredo** *m.* • (lit.): tangle, snarl (in wool).

SYNONYM -8: **follón** *m.* • (lit.): lazy, idle.

SYNONYM -9: **garrón** *m. (Argentina).*

SYNONYM -10: **golpaso** *m. (Mexico)* • (lit.): heavy or violent blow.

SYNONYM -11: **jaleo** *m.* • (lit.): noisy party.

SYNONYM -12: **kilombo** *m. (Argentina).*

SYNONYM -13: **lío** *m.* • (lit.): bundle, package.

SYNONYM -14: **marrón** *m. (Spain).*

SYNONYM -15: **mogollón** *m.*

SYNONYM -16: **paquete** *m. (Cuba)* • (lit.): package.

SYNONYM -17: **revoltijo** *m.* • (lit.): jumble, mix-up.

SYNONYM -18: **revoltillo** *m.* • (lit.): jumble, mix-up.

SYNONYM -19: **revuelo** *m. (Cuba)* • (lit.): second flight.

ALSO: **revoltillo de huevos** *m.* scrambled eggs • (lit.): a jumble of eggs.

SYNONYM -20: **sángano** *m. (Puerto Rico).*

lana *f. (Spain)* money • (lit.): wool.

example: Se nota que Javier tiene **lana**. Siempre conduce un automóvil último modelo.

translation: You can tell Javier has **money**. He always drives a late-model car.

SYNONYM -1: **guita** *f.* *(Argentina)* • (lit.): twine.

SYNONYM -2: **pasta** *f.* • (lit.): pasta, paste.

SYNONYM -3: **plata** *f.* • (lit.): silver.

SYNONYM -4: **tela** *f.* *(Argentina)* • (lit.): material, cloth, fabric.

mangante *m.* thief.

example: Anoche entró un **mangante** a mi casa y se llevó mis joyas.

translation: Last night a **thief** broke into my house and stole my jewelry.

SYNONYM -1: **caco** *m.* • (lit.): thief.

SYNONYM -2: **chorizo** *m.* • (lit.): a type of Spanish sausage.

SYNONYM -3: **chorro** *m.* *(Argentina)*.

SYNONYM -4: **pillo** *m.* *(Puerto Rico)*.

SYNONYM -5: **ratero** *m.* *(Mexico)* • (lit.): petty thief.

mangar *v.* to steal, to rob.

example: Ese tipo quiso **robar** el banco pero lo atrapó la policía.

translation: That guy tried to **rob** the bank but he was caught by the police.

SYNONYM -1: **afanar** *v.* *(Argentina)* • **1.** to steal, to swipe • **2.** to work hard (as seen earlier).

SYNONYM -2: **escamotear** *v.*

SYNONYM -3: **hurtar** *v.*

pez gordo *m.* person of great importance, "big wig" • (lit.): fat fish.

example: Algún día yo seré el **pez gordo** de esta compañía.

translation: Someday I'll be the **big cheese** in this company.

SYNONYM: **de peso** *adj.* • (lit.): of weight, weighty.

example: Ese señor es una persona **de peso**.

translation: That man's a **big wig**.

poli *f.* a popular abbreviation for *policía* meaning "police," or "cops."

example: ¡Corre que viene la **poli**!

translation: Run! The **cops** are coming!

SYNONYM -1: **cana** *f. (Argentina).*

SYNONYM -2: **chota** *f.*

talego *m.* jail, prison.

example: ¡Si sigues portándote así vas a acabar en el **talego**!

translation: If you continue to behave that way, you're going to end up in **jail**!

SYNONYM -1: **bote** *m.* • (lit.): rowboat.

SYNONYM -2: **cana** *f. (Argentina)* • **1.** prison, "slammer" • **2.** police (as seen earlier).

SYNONYM -3: **fondo** *m. (Puerto Rico)* • (lit.): the bottom.

NOTE: **acabar en el talego / bote** *exp.* to end up in jail, in the "slammer."

trastornado/a (estar) *adj.* to be furious, angry.

example: El jefe está **trastornado** porque Pepe no terminó el trabajo.

translation: The boss is **furious** because Pepe didn't finish his job.

SYNONYM -1: **cabreado/a** *adj.* (to be) all worked up (over something).

ALSO: **agarrar / pillar un cabreo** *exp.* to fly off the handle.

SYNONYM -2: **pusarse loco/a** *exp. (Puerto Rico)* to cause to go crazy (with anger).

SYNONYM -3: **rabioso/a** *adj.* • (lit.): rabid (or full of rabies).

Practice the Vocabulary

(Answers to Lesson 3, p. 174)

A. Fill in the blank with the appropriate word(s) using the list below.

ascuas (en)	**currar**	**lana**
besugo	**enchufe**	**pez gordo**
chorrada	**fichado**	**poli**
colmo	**gazpacho**	**trastornado**

1. Aquí no hay organización. Esto es un verdadero ______________ .
2. ¡Esto es el _______ ! Javier siempre quiere comer gratis en mi casa.
3. María está _________ . Parece que va a tener un ataque de nervios.
4. Por ahí viene el ____________ . Seguro que nos manda hacer algo.
5. David está muy ______________ hoy porque todo le ha salido mal.
6. Jorge está muy contento porque gana mucho dinero en su ______________ .
7. Parece que el jefe tiene ______________ a Marcos.
8. Hoy estoy muy cansado. No tengo ganas de ______________ .
9. Voy a llamar a la ______________ porque ese tipo está muy violento.
10. No me puedo creer que Luis hizo una ______________ como esa.
11. ¡Mira que coche tan caro tiene Alfonso! Parece que tiene mucha ____________ .
12. José es un ______________ . Siempre está haciendo tonterías.

B. Match the Spanish with the English translation by writing the corresponding letter of the answer in the box.

☐ 1. I'll bet that it snows on Pedro's birthday.

☐ 2. I love working at the airport.

☐ 3. Carlos is a gossip.

☐ 4. I can't believe you would do such a stupid thing.

☐ 5. I'm so glad they finally caught that thief.

☐ 6. Slow down! I see cops at that corner.

☐ 7. That guy is going to end up in jail.

☐ 8. I can't believe someone stole my wallet.

☐ 9. Ana is on pins and needles.

☐ 10. Andrés is such an idiot.

☐ 11. This takes the cake!

☐ 12. My dad is furious because I took his car last night.

A. **Mi papá está trastornado porque me llevé su coche anoche.**

B. **Ana está en ascuas.**

C. **¡Más despacio! Veo a la poli en la esquina.**

D. **A que nieva en el cumpleaños de Pedro.**

E. **Me encanta currar en el aeropuerto.**

F. **No me puedo creer que alguien se mangó mi cartera.**

G. **No me puedo creer que tú harías una chorrada como esa.**

H. **Andrés es un besugo.**

I. **¡Esto es el colmo!**

J. **Carlos es un cuentista.**

K. **Estoy contento de que por fin atraparon a ese mangante.**

L. **Ese tipo va a acabar en el talego.**

C. CROSSWORD

Fill in the crossword puzzle on the opposite page by choosing the correct words from the list below.

ascuas	**currar**	**mangante**
besugo	**enchufe**	**mangar**
chico	**fichado**	**poli**
chorrada	**gazpacho**	**talego**
colmo	**gordo**	**trastornado**
cuentista	**lana**	

ACROSS

12. ___________ *f.* money • (lit.): wool.

19. ___________ *f.* police, "cops."

22. ___________ *f.* stupid or despicable act.

23. ___________ *exp.* to take the cake, to be the last straw.

32. ___________ *m.* mess, predicament, jam • (lit.): a type of Spanish tomato soup.

39. ___________ *m.&f.* gossip • (lit.): story teller.

44. ___________ *adj.* to be on someone's bad side, to be on someone's bad list • (lit.): to be posted or affixed.

48. ___________ *m.* jail, prison.

54. ___________ *m.* thief.

DOWN

3. **pez** ___________ *m.* person of great importance, "big wig" • (lit.): fat fish.

6. ___________ *m.* idiot, fool, harebrained person, scatterbrain • (lit.): sea bream (a kind of fish).

13. ___________ *exp.* to be on pins and needles.

15. ___________ *m.* guy, "dude."

18. ___________ *adj.* to be furious, angry.

35. ___________ *m.* cushy job • (lit.): plug, socket.

38. ___________ *v.* to steal, to rob.

45. ___________ *v.* to work.

CROSSWORD

3 6 12 13 15 18 19 22 23 32 35 38 39 44 45 48 54

D. Underline the appropriate word(s) that best complete(s) the phrase.

1. Aquel muchacho no sabe nada. Es un (**besucón**, **besugo**, **beato**).

2. Luis siempre está diciendo mentiras. Es un (**cuentero**, **cuentagotas**, **cuentista**).

3. Me gusta mucho (**currar**, **culpar**, **contar**) en la biblioteca.

4. ¡Esto es el (**colombo**, **color**, **colmo**)!

5. Darío consiguió trabajo porque tenía un buen (**encargo**, **enchufe**, **estufa**).

6. La (**polo**, **poli**, **pala**) llegó muy pronto al accidente.

7. Ese tipo se porta tan mal que va a acabar en el (**taladro**, **tabarra**, **talego**).

8. Se nota que Manuel tiene mucha (**lana**, **lona**, **lata**).

9. Esta universidad está muy desorganizada. Es un verdadero (**galardón**, **gallito**, **gazpacho**).

10. El profesor está (**transferido**, **trastornado**, **tragado**) porque nadie fue a su clase.

11. ¡Empieza a trabajar! Por ahí viene el (**pez gordo**, **perro flaco**, **tiburón**).

12. Ese (**chaco**, **chano**, **chico**) es muy simpático.

E. DICTATION
Test Your Aural Comprehension

(This dictation can be found in the Appendix on page 190.)

If you are following along with your cassette, you will now hear a series of sentences from the opening dialogue. These sentences will be read by a native speaker at normal conversational speed (which may seem fast to you at first). In addition, the words will be pronounced *as you would actually hear them in a conversation,* oftentimes including some common reductions.

The first time the sentences are presented, simply listen in order to get accustomed to the speed and heavy use of reductions. The sentences will then be read again with a pause after each to give you time to write down what you heard. The third time the sentences are read, follow along with what you have written.

LECCIÓN CUATRO

Mi *media naranja* y yo estamos celebrando nuestro aniversario.

*(trans.): My **wife** and I are celebrating our anniversary.*
*(lit.): My **half an orange** and I are celebrating our anniversary.*

Lección Cuatro

Dialogue in Slang

Mi media naranja y yo estamos celebrando nuestro aniversario.

Marco: ¡Oye mi **cuate**! ¿**Qué hay de nuevo**? Pareces **amuermado** hoy.

Jaime: No, lo que pasa es que estoy **agotado** porque he tenido que **chambear** tarde toda la semana. Estoy tratando de ganar más **plata** para poder comprarle un regalo de aniversario muy especial a mi **media naranja**. Le voy a comprar un boleto para que vaya a Madrid a visitar a sus **viejos**.

Marco: ¡Qué **rechulo**! ¡Eso si que es un regalo **morrocotudo**! Espero que sepa lo **suertuda** que es de tener un **hombre** como tú.

Jaime: ¡Por supuesto! ¡Yo se lo digo todos los días! Afortunadamente, he conseguido un buen **chollo** con el boleto de avión. No quiero que pienses que soy un **buitre**, pero si puedo ahorrar un poco de **plata**, ¿por qué no?

Marco: Bueno, para celebrar tu aniversario, voy a pagar tu **cuentón**.

Jaime: ¡**Vale**! Me alegro de que vinieras hoy. ¡Qué **chorra** he tenido!

Lesson Four

Marco: Hey **buddy**! **What's new**? You look **a little out of it** today.

Jaime: No, it's just that I'm **exhausted** because I had to **work** late all week. I'm trying to make extra **money** to buy my **wife** a special anniversary gift. I'm buying her a ticket to go visit her **folks** in Madrid.

Marco: **Cool**! That's an **awesome** gift! I hope she knows what a **lucky person** she is to have a **husband** like you.

Jaime: Of course! I tell her that every day! Fortunately, I'm getting a great **deal** on the airplane ticket. I don't want you to think that I'm a **cheapskate**, but if I can save a few **bucks**, why not?

Marco: Well, to celebrate your anniversary, I'm going to pay your **tab**.

Jaime: **You got a deal**! I'm so glad you came here today. What **luck** for me!

Vocabulary

agotado/a (estar) *adj.* to be exhausted, completely tired out • (lit.): to be emptied or drained.

example: He trabajado toda la noche. Estoy **agotado**.

translation: I worked all night long. I'm **pooped**.

SYNONYM -1: **como un trapo viejo (estar / sentirse)** *exp.* • (lit.): to be/to feel like an old rag.

SYNONYM -2: **hecho polvo (estar)** *exp.* • (lit.): to be made of dust.

SYNONYM -3: **muerto/a (estar)** *adj.* • (lit.): to be dead.

SYNONYM -4: **rendido/a (estar)** *adj.* • (lit.): to be rendered (all off one's energy).

SYNONYM -5: **reventado/a (estar)** *adj.* • (lit.): to be burst (like a balloon whose air has been suddenly let out).

amuermado/a (estar) *adj.* to be out of it, dazed.

example: Parece que Luis no durmió bien anoche. Hoy está **amuermado**.

translation: It looks like Luis didn't sleep well last night. He's **out of it** today.

SYNONYM -1: **aplantanado/a** *adj.*

SYNONYM -2: **aturdido/a** *adj.*

SYNONYM -3: **volando/a** *adj. (Argentina).*

buitre *m.* • **1.** cheapskate • **2.** opportunist • (lit.): vulture.

example (1): Jorge es tan **buitre** que nunca desayuna para ahorrar dinero.

translation: Jorge is such a **cheapskate** that he never eats breakfast just so that he can save money.

example (2): Julio es un **buitre**. Cuando perdí mi trabajo, en vez de ayudarme, intentó conseguir mi trabado.

translation: Julio is a real **opportunist**. When I lost my job, instead of helping me, he tried to get my old job.

SYNONYM: **amarrete** *m. (Argentina).*

chambear *v.* to work.

example: Hoy no tengo ganas de **chambear**. Estoy muy cansado.

translation: Today I don't feel like **working**. I'm really tired.

NOTE: **chamba** *f.* job.

SYNONYM -1: **currar** *v. (Spain).*

SYNONYM -2: **doblar el lomo** *exp. (Puerto Rico)* to work hard • (lit.): to fold one's back in two.

chollo *m.* good deal.

example: Solo pagué 300 dólares por este automóvil. ¡Qué **chollo**!

translation: I only paid $300 for this car. What a **deal**!

SYNONYM -1: **buena ganga (una)** *f. (Puerto Rico).*

SYNONYM -2: **curro** *m. (Argentina).*

chorra *f.* good luck.

example: ¡No te puedes imaginar la **chorra** que he tenido! ¡Me tocó la lotería!

translation: You won't believe my **luck**! I won the lottery!

ALSO: **tener chorra** *exp.* to be lucky.

cuate *m. (Mexico)* buddy, friend • (lit.): twin.

example: Alfredo es mi **cuate**. Siempre puedo contar con él.

translation: Alfredo is my **buddy**. I can always count on him.

SYNONYM -1: **amigote** *m.* • (lit.): big friend (from the noun *amigo*).

SYNONYM -2: **camarada** *m.* • (lit.): comrade.

SYNONYM -3: **carnal** *m.* • (lit.): related by blood.

SYNONYM -4: **compadre** *m.* • (lit.): godfather.

SYNONYM -5: **hermano** *m.* • (lit.): brother.

SYNONYM -6: **jefe** *m.* • (lit.): boss.

SYNONYM -7: **mano** *m.*

NOTE: This is a shortened version of *hermano* meaning "brother."

SYNONYM -8: **tío** *m. (Cuba / Spain)* • (lit.): uncle.

cuentón *m.* • **1.** big bill, check • **2.** long story.

example (1): ¡Casi me da un ataque cardíaco cuando me llegó el **cuentón** y me di cuenta cuanto costaba comer en ese restaurante!

translation: I almost had a heart attack when I got the **check** and found out how much our meal cost at the restaurant!

example (2): Si quieres, te cuento lo que me pasó hoy en la escuela pero es un **cuentón**.

translation: If you want, I'll tell you what happened to me at school today but it's a **long story**.

SYNONYM -1: **dolorosa** *f. (Puerto Rico)* • (lit.): that which causes pain (from the masculine noun *dolor* meaning "pain").

SYNONYM -2: **importe** *m.*

SYNONYM -3: **monto** *m.*

NOTE: The synonyms above apply to definition **1** only.

ANTONYM: **cuentecilla** *f.* small bill or check.

hombre • **1.** *m.* husband • **2.** *interj.* wow! • (lit.): man.

example (1): No me puedo quejar. Mi **hombre** me trata muy bien.

translation: I can't complain. My **husband** treats me very well.

example (2): ¡**Hombre**! ¡Esta mujer es guapísima!

translation: **Wow**! That girl is beautiful!

SYNONYM: **tipo** *m. (Argentina).*

SEE -1: **media naranja** *(next entry).*

SEE -2: **¡Hombre!**, *p. 72.*

media naranja *exp.* better half, spouse • (lit.): **1.** half an orange • **2.** dome, cupola.

example: A mi **media naranja** y a mí nos encanta ir a México de vacaciones.

translation: My **wife** and I love going to Mexico on vacation.

NOTE -1: In Spanish, a dome is called a *media naranja* (literally, "half an orange") due to its shape.

NOTE -2: *Media naranja* is commonly used as a humorous and affectionate term for one's spouse, since one half completes the other as would two halves of an orange.

SYNONYM: **jermu** *f. Argentina)* a reverse transformation of the word *mujer* (jer-mu) meaning woman or wife.

morrocotudo/a *adj.* • **1.** neat, cool, terrific, fabulous • **2.** very important • **3.** difficult • **4.** wealthy • **5.** big, enormous.

example (1): El nuevo automóvil de Carlos es muy **morrocotudo**.

translation: Carlos' new car is really **cool**.

example (2): Mi entrevista con el presidente es **morrocotuda**.

translation: My interview with the President is **very important**.

example (3): Este problema de matemáticas es **morrocotudo**.

translation: This math problem is very **difficult**.

example (4): Pablo es un **morrocotudo**. ¡Debes de ver la casa nueva que se ha comprado!

translation: Pablo is very **wealthy**. You should see the new house he bought!

example (5): ¡Ese barco es **morrocotudo**!

translation: That ship is **enormous**!

NOTE: The following are synonyms for example (1) only:

SYNONYM -1: **alucinante** *adj. (Argentina).*

SYNONYM -2: **chulo/a** *adj. (Spain)* neat, cool, terrific.

SYNONYM -3: **del carah** *adj. (Puerto Rico).*

SYNONYM -4: **molón** *adj. (Spain).*

ANTONYM: **chungo/a** *adj.* ugly, "uncool."

NOTE: This is an antonym for the previous example (1) only.

plata *f.* money • (lit.): silver.

example: En los Estados Unidos los jugadores de baloncesto ganan mucha **plata**.

translation: In the U.S., basketball players make a lot of **money**.

SYNONYMS: SEE - **lana**, *p. 39*.

ALSO: **podrido/a de dinero (estar)** *exp.* to be rich • to be rolling in money • (lit.): to be rotten in money.

NOTE: Any synonym for *dinero* may be substituted.

¿Qué hay de nuevo? *exp.* What's new? • (lit.): [same].

example: ¿**Qué hay de nuevo** Sergio? ¡Hace tiempo que no te veo!

translation: **What's new**, Sergio? It's been a long time!

NOTE: **de nuevo** *adv.* again.

example: Lo hizo **de nuevo**.

translation: He / She did it again.

SYNONYM -1: **¿Qué onda?** *exp.* • (lit.): What wave?

SYNONYM -2: **¿Qué haces, papá?** *exp.* *(Argentina)* What are you up to, pal? • (lit.): What are you doing, pops?

SYNONYM -3: **¿Qué hubo?** *exp.* • (lit.): What was? / What had?

rechulo/a *adj.* very "cool," neat.

example: Este libro está **rechulo**.

translation: This book is really **cool**.

NOTE: In Spanish, it is very popular to attach the prefix "*re*" to the beginning of an adjective for greater emphasis:
bonito = beautiful • ***re****bonito* = really beautiful
fuerte = strong • ***re****fuerte* = really strong, etc.

SYNONYM -1: **¡Qué chévere!** *interj. (Puerto Rico).*

SYNONYM -2: **¡Qué grande!** *interj. (Argentina).*

SYNONYM -3: **¡Qué guay!** *interj. (Spain).*

suertudo/a *adj.* lucky person.

example: Paco es un **suertudo**. Ya ha ganado la lotería dos veces.

translation: Paco is such a **lucky person**. He won the lottery twice already.

vale *interj.* okay, "you got a deal" • (lit.): worth.

example: ¿Quieres ir al cine conmigo?
¡**Vale**!

translation: Do you want to go to the movies with me?
Okay!

NOTE: This interjection comes from the verb *valer* meaning "to have worth."

ALSO: ¡**Sí vale**! *interj.* Why, yes!

SYNONYM -1: **genial** *adj. (Argentina).*

SYNONYM -2: **OK** *interj.*

NOTE: This interjection has been borrowed from English and is becoming increasingly popular throughout the Spanish-speaking countries.

viejos *m.pl.* parents, folks • (lit.): the old ones.

example: Me encanta ir a casa de mis **viejos** porque siempre hay algo bueno de comer.

translation: I love going to my **folks** because there is always something good to eat.

NOTE -1: **viejo** *m.* • **1.** father • **2.** husband • (lit.): old man.

NOTE -2: **vieja** *f.* • **1.** mother • **2.** wife • (lit.): old woman.

Practice the Vocabulary

(Answers to Lesson 4, p. 176)

A. Choose the letter corresponding to the correct definition of the word(s) in boldface.

1. **chambear**:
   a. to sign
   b. to work

2. **buitre**:
   a. big spender
   b. cheapskate

3. **agotado (estar)**:
   a. to be exhausted
   b. to be wide awake

4. **chollo**:
   a. a bad deal
   b. a good deal

5. **suertudo**:
   a. a stupid person
   b. a lucky person

6. **vale**:
   a. okay
   b. cartera

7. **viejos**:
   a. kids
   b. parents

8. **plata**:
   a. a very thin person
   b. money

9. **amuermado (estar)**:
   a. to be out of it
   b. to be alert

10. **chorra**:
    a. misfortune
    b. good luck

11. **rechulo**:
    a. ugly
    b. cool

12. **cuentón**:
    a. a big bill
    b. friend

B. Fill in the following blanks with the letter that corresponds to the best answer.

1. Alfredo es mi mejor ________. Siempre vamos juntos a todas partes.
   a. **cuadro** b. **cohete** c. **cuate**

2. No me puedo quejar. Mi ________ siempre se acuerda de nuestro aniversario.
   a. **hombro** b. **hombre** c. **hombrón**

3. ¡Me encanta tu auto! Es muy ________.
   a. **morrocotudo** b. **morrudo** c. **motilón**

4. ¡Me encanta salir por la noche con mi ________!
   a. **medio melón** b. **medio aguacate** c. **media naranja**

5. Parece que Jorge tiene mucha ________. ¡Mira qué coche tan caro tiene!
   a. **arena** b. **oro** c. **plata**

6. ¡Buenos días! ¿Qué ________?
   a. **hay de nuevo** b. **de adiós** c. **hay de viejo**

7. Mi hermano y yo vamos a visitar a nuestros ________ en Madrid.
   a. **vidrios** b. **viejos** c. **viudos**

8. Estoy ________ porque he tenido que trabajar tarde toda la semana.
   a. **viejo** b. **zote** c. **agotado**

9. Hoy tuve que ________ doce horas en mi trabajo.
   a. **chabolar** b. **chambear** c. **chapar**

10. Cuando fui a comer a ese restaurante con Manuel, tuve que pagar el ________ .
    a. **cuentón** b. **cuento** c. **historia**

11. José es un ________. Siempre gana cuando apuesta.
    a. **sufrido** b. **suertudo** c. **servidor**

12. ¿Quieres ir al cine conmigo? Sí, ________.
    a. **valgo** b. **valet** c. **vale**

C. Match the Spanish with the English translation by writing the corresponding letter of the answer in the box.

☐ 1. That's an awesome gift!

☐ 2. Andrés is my best buddy.

☐ 3. I'm so glad I bought this car. What a deal!

☐ 4. My husband gave me flowers last night.

☐ 5. What's new, Rodolfo?

☐ 6. I love your dress. It's so cool!

☐ 7. Yesterday, I went to visit my parents.

☐ 8. He seems to have a lot of money.

☐ 9. Look at Javier! He's out of it today.

☐ 10. I can't believe I have to work tonight.

☐ 11. I've worked all day long. I'm exhausted!

☐ 12. Okay. I'll go with you.

A. **Me encanta tu vestido. ¡Es rechulo!**

B. **Ayer fui a visitar a mis viejos.**

C. **¿Qué hay de nuevo, Rodolfo?**

D. **¡Eso si que es un regalo morrocotudo!**

E. **No me puedo creer que tengo que chambear esta noche.**

F. **Parece que tiene mucha plata.**

G. **¡Mira Javier! Está amuermado hoy.**

H. **Andrés es mi mejor cuate.**

I. **Me alegro de haber comprado este auto. ¡Qué chollo!**

J. **Mi hombre me dio flores anoche.**

K. **¡Vale! Iré contigo.**

L. **He currado todo el día. ¡Estoy agotado!**

D. WORD SEARCH

Using the list below, circle the words in the grid on the opposite page that fit the following expressions. Words may be spelled up, down, or across.

agotado	**cuate**	**nuevo**
amuermado	**cuentón**	**rechulo**
buitre	**hombre**	**suertudo**
chambear	**naranja**	**Vale**
chollo	**morrocotudo**	**viejos**
chorra	**plata**	

1. __________ **(estar)** *adj.* to be exhausted, completely tired out • (lit.): to be emptied or drained.
2. __________ **(estar)** *adj.* to be out of it, dazed.
3. __________ *m.* • **1.** cheapskate • **2.** opportunist • (lit.): vulture.
4. __________ *v.* to work.
5. __________ *m.* good deal.
6. __________ *f.* good luck.
7. __________ *m.* buddy, friend.
8. __________ *m.* • **1.** big bill, check • **2.** long story.
9. __________ • **1.** *m.* husband • **2.** *interj.* wow! • (lit.): man.
10. **media** __________ *exp.* better half, spouse • (lit.): **1.** half an orange • **2.** dome, cupola.
11. __________ *adj.* • **1.** neat, cool, terrific, fabulous • **2.** very important • **3.** difficult • **4.** wealthy • **5.** big, enormous.
12. __________ *f.* money • (lit.): silver.
13. **¿Qué hay de __________?** *exp.* What's new? • (lit.): [same].
14. __________ *adj.* very "cool," neat.
15. __________ *adj.* lucky person.

16. __________ *interj*. okay, "you got a deal" • (lit.): worth.

17. __________ *m.pl.* parents, folks • (lit.): the old ones.

FIND-A-WORD PUZZLE

D	S	Y	O	N	A	E	A	T	J	W	E
O	A	G	O	T	A	D	O	O	A	A	S
N	T	J	M	E	D	S	U	M	D	S	M
D	O	O	A	M	U	E	R	M	A	D	O
A	U	U	A	Q	K	N	C	N	T	E	R
J	C	R	C	U	E	N	T	Ó	N	R	R
E	H	S	H	E	A	A	A	H	S	C	O
C	A	D	O	S	L	R	N	E	C	H	C
D	M	E	M	P	L	A	T	A	A	E	O
U	B	J	B	A	A	N	R	H	R	N	T
O	E	E	R	N	H	J	C	H	E	N	U
W	A	V	E	S	E	A	E	K	E	U	D
Q	R	A	M	M	H	R	L	N	S	C	O
C	T	I	U	O	T	E	S	U	W	H	C
V	A	S	S	N	H	C	E	E	I	O	U
B	U	I	T	R	E	H	E	V	L	R	A
H	R	V	E	I	S	U	I	O	L	R	T
U	E	A	P	T	I	L	T	L	W	A	E
C	H	O	L	L	O	O	H	Y	O	A	O

E. DICTATION
Test Your Aural Comprehension

(This dictation can be found in the Appendix on page 190.)

If you are following along with your cassette, you will now hear a series of sentences from the opening dialogue. These sentences will be read by a native speaker at normal conversational speed (which may seem fast to you at first). In addition, the words will be pronounced *as you would actually hear them in a conversation,* oftentimes including some common reductions.

The first time the sentences are presented, simply listen in order to get accustomed to the speed and heavy use of reductions. The sentences will then be read again with a pause after each to give you time to write down what you heard. The third time the sentences are read, follow along with what you have written.

LECCIÓN CINCO

¡Esta chica es un verdadero *merengue*!

(trans.): That girl's a real ***babe****!*
(lit.): That girl's a real ***meringue****!*

Dialogue in Slang

¡Esta chica es un verdadero merengue!

Esperanza: ¡**Hombre**! Cuando te **arreglas** te ves bellísima. Los chicos van a pensar que eres un verdadero **merengue** cuando te vean en la **tertulia** de esta noche. Espero que no creas que soy un **comecocos**, pero ese vestido es una **chulada**. Es mucho más bonito que el vestido que te pusiste antes. Parecías un **escuincle**.

Irene: Tienes razón. Pero este me encanta. De hecho, creo que también voy a comprar el bolso y los zapatos que van con este vestido. No quiero venir con toda la **trupe**, así que voy a comprarlos ahora y voy a **pagar al contado**. Espero que no se me ensucie. La última vez que me puse algo caro para ir a una fiesta, un **adoquín** derramó comida encima mía.

Esperanza: No te **comas el coco** tanto. Además, si ves que tiene un poquito de **mugre**, lo puedes lavar.

Lesson Five

Esperanza: **Man**! When you **fix yourself up**, you look gorgeous. Guys are going to think you're a real **babe** when they see you at the **get-together** tonight. I hope you don't think I'm **trying to push my opinions on you**, but that dress is so **cool**. It's so much prettier than the first dress you tried on. It made you look like a **little kid**.

Irene: You're right. But I love this one. In fact, I think I'll buy the matching purse and shoes, too. I don't want to have to come back here with the whole **gang** (meaning "the whole family"), so I'm going to buy them now and **pay cash**. I just hope I can keep it clean. The last time I wore something expensive to a party, some **jerk** spilled food on me.

Esperanza: Don't **get all worked up about it**. Besides, if you get a little **dirt** on it, you can always have it cleaned.

Vocabulary

adoquín *m.* jerk, fool, moron, simpleton • (lit.): paving block.

example: Julio es un **adoquín**. Siempre está diciendo estupideces.

translation: Julio is a **jerk**. He's always talking nonsense.

SYNONYM -1: **boludo** *m. (Argentina).*

SYNONYM -2: **bruto/a** *adj.* • (lit.): stupid, crude.

SYNONYM -3: **caballo** *m. (Puerto Rico).*

SYNONYM -4: **cabezota** *adj.*

NOTE: This comes from the feminine noun *cabeza* meaning "head." The suffix *-ota* is commonly used to modify the meaning of a noun; in this case, changing it to "big head."

SYNONYM -5: **cateto/a** *adj. (Spain).*

SYNONYM -6: **chorlito** *m.* • (lit.): golden plover (which is a kind of bird).

SYNONYM -7: **goma** *f. (Argentina)* • (lit.): rubber, glue.

SYNONYM -8: **matado/a** *n. (Spain)* idiot or nerd.

SYNONYM -9: **menso/a** *n. (Mexico).*

SYNONYM -10: **pendejo** *m. (Argentina)* • **1.** idiot, imbecile • **2.** coward • (lit.): public hair.

SYNONYM -11: **soquete** *m. (Cuba).*

SYNONYM -12: **tarado/a** *adj. (Argentina).*

SYNONYM -13: **tosco/a** *adj.* • (lit.): coarse, crude, unrefined.

SYNONYM -14: **zopenco/a** *adj.* • (lit.): dull, stupid.

ANTONYM -1: **avispado/a** *adj.* • (lit.): clever, sharp.

NOTE: This comes from the term *avispa* meaning "wasp."

ANTONYM -2: **despabilado/a** *adj.* • (lit.): awakened.

NOTE: This comes from the verb *despavilar* meaning "to wake up."

ANTONYM -3: **despejado/a** *adj.* • (lit.): confident, assured (in behavior), clear (as in a cloudless sky).

ANTONYM -4: **listillo/a** *adj.* • (lit.): a small clever person.

NOTE: This comes from the adjective *listo/a* meaning "ready" or "clever."

ANTONYM -5: **pillo** *adj.* • (lit.): roguish, mischievous.

NOTE: This adjective is always used in the masculine form. Interestingly enough, the feminine form, *pilla*, is rarely ever seen.

ANTONYM -6: **vivo/a** *adj.* • (lit.): alive.

arreglarse *v.* to fix oneself up, to make oneself look attractive • (lit.): to fix oneself up (from the verb *arreglar* meaning "to repair something").

example: María está guapísima cuando **se arregla**.

translation: Maria is beautiful when she **fixes herself up**.

ALSO -1: **arreglarse con** *exp.* to conform to, to agree with, to come to an agreement with.

ALSO -2: **arreglárselas** *v.* to manage.

SYNONYM -1: **empaquetarse** *v.* *(Puerto Rico).*

SYNONYM -2: **pintarse** *v.* • (lit.): to paint oneself.

chulada *f.* said of something "cool," neat.

example: ¡Este automóvil es una verdadera **chulada**!

translation: This car is so **cool**!

SYNONYM -1: **copado/a** *adj. (Argentina).*

SYNONYM -2: **rebueno/a** *adj. (Argentina).*

SYNONYM -3: **tumba (estar que)** *exp. (Puerto Rico)* • (lit.): to fall (for).

ANTONYM: **chungo/a** *adj.* "uncool," ugly, lousy.

comerse el coco *exp.* • **1.** to worry, to get all worked up about something • **2.** to convince someone to do something • (lit.): to eat someone's head (since the masculine noun *coco,* literally meaning "coconut," is used in Spanish slang to mean "head" or "noggin").

example (1): No **te comas el coco**. Mañana será otro día.

translation: Don't **get all worked up about it**. Tomorrow will be a new beginning.

example (2): Voy a **comerle el coco** a Javier para que me dé dinero.

translation: I'm going to **convince** Javier to give me some money.

SYNONYM -1: **darse manija** *exp. (Argentina)* • (lit.): to give oneself a handle.

SYNONYM -2: **perder la cabeza** *exp. (Cuba)* • (lit.): to lose one's head.

SYNONYM -3: **rascar el coco** *exp. (Mexico)* • (lit.): to scratch one's head or "coconut."

comecocos *m.* a person who tries to push his/her opinion on others.

example: Javier es un **comecocos**. Piensa que lo que le gusta a él, le debe gustar a todos.

translation: Javier always **tries to push his opinion on others**. He thinks that whatever he likes, everybody should like, too.

SYNONYM -1: **comebolas** *m. (Cuba).*

SYNONYM -2: **rollo** *m. (Spain)* • (lit.): roll.

escuincle *m.* little kid, small child.

example: ¡No me lo puedo creer! Luisa ya tiene siete **escuincles** y ¡está embarazada otra vez!

translation: I can't believe it! Luisa already has seven **kids** and she's pregnant again!

SYNONYM -1: **chiquillo/a** *n.*

NOTE: This noun comes from the adjective *chico/a* meaning "small."

SYNONYM -2: **chiquitín/a** *n.*

NOTE: This noun comes from the adjective *chico/a* meaning "small."

SYNONYM -3: **crío/a** *m. (Spain)* • (lit.): a nursing-baby.

SYNONYM -4: **gurrumino/a** *n.* • (lit.): weak or sickly person, "whimp."

SYNONYM -5: **mocoso/a** *n.* • (lit.): snotty-nosed person.

SYNONYM -6: **nené** *m. (Puerto Rico / Cuba).*

NOTE: By putting an accent over the second "e" in *nene*, this standard term for "baby" acquires a slang connotation.

SYNONYM -7: **párvulo** *m.* • (lit.): tot.

SYNONYM -8: **pequeñajo/a** *n.*

NOTE: This noun comes from the adjective *pequeño/a* meaning "small."

SYNONYM -9: **pituso/a** *n.* smurf (from the cartoon characters).

ANTONYM -1: **grandote** *m.*

NOTE: This noun comes from the adjective *grande* meaning "big."

ANTONYM -2: **grandullón/a** *n.* big kid.

NOTE: This noun comes from the adjective *grande* meaning "big."

¡Hombre! *interj.* Man alive! For crying outloud! Wow! • (lit.): man!

example: ¡**Hombre**! Claro que quiero ser millonario!

translation: **Man**! Of course I want to become a millionaire!

SYNONYM -1: **¡Ay Caray!** *interj. (Cuba).*

SYNONYM -2: **¡Caballero!** *interj.* • (lit.): Sir!

SYNONYM -3: **¡Che!** *interj. (Argentina).*

SYNONYM -4: **¡Guau!** *interj. (Spain / Puerto Rico* - pronounced *Wow!*).

VARIATION: **¡Guao!**

SYNONYM -5: **¡Manitas!** *interj. (Puerto Rico).*

SYNONYM -6: **¡Mujer!** *interj. (Cuba)* • (lit.): woman.

SYNONYM -7: **¡Tío!** *interj.* • (lit.): Uncle!

SYNONYM -8: **¡Ufa!** *interj. (Argentina).*

merengue *m.* beautiful woman, "knockout" • (lit.): meringue, a type of pie.

example: Ana es la chica más guapa de la escuela. ¡Es un verdadero **merengue**!

translation: Ana is the most beautiful girl at school. She's a real **babe**!

SYNONYM -1: **bollito** *m. (Spain)* • (lit.): a small sweet cake.

SYNONYM -2: **bombón** *m.* bonbon • (lit.): (a type of chocolate candy).

SYNONYM -3: **buena moza** *f.* • (lit.): good maid.

SYNONYM -4: **buenona** *f.*

NOTE: This noun comes from the adjective *bueno/a* meaning "good."

SYNONYM -5: **diosa** *f. (Argentina)* godess.

SYNONYM -6: **maja** *f.* • (lit.): flashy or showy.

SYNONYM -7: **mamasíta** *f.* • (lit.): little mother.

SYNONYM -8: **pimpollo** *m.* • (lit.): flower bud or bloom.

SYNONYM -9: **tía buena** *f. (Spain / Cuba)* • (lit.): good aunt.

SYNONYM -10: **venus** *f.* • (lit.): Venus (the goddess of beauty).

mugre *f.* filth, grime, dirt.

example: ¡Oye Paco! Tu automóvil está lleno de **mugre**. ¡Parece que nunca lo lavas!

translation: Hey Paco! Your car is so full of **dirt**. It looks like you never wash it!

SYNONYM -1: **cochambre** *f.* • (lit.): greasy.

SYNONYM -2: **porquería** *f.* • (lit.): junk.

pagar al contado *exp.* to pay cash on the barrel • (lit.): to pay counted.

example: Cuando como en un restaurante, siempre intento **pagar al contado** en lugar de con tarjeta de crédito.

translation: When I eat at a restaurant, I always try to **pay cash** instead of using my credit card.

SYNONYM -1: **pagar a tocateja** *exp.* • (lit.): to pay to the touch.

SYNONYM -2: **pagar con billetes** *exp.* • (lit.): to pay with bills.

tertulia *f.* social gathering, "get-together."

example: Todos los sábados por la noche tenemos una **tertulia** en casa de Ramón.

translation: Every Saturday night, we have a **get-together** at Ramon's house.

ALSO: **tertulia (estar de)** *exp.* to talk, to chat.

SYNONYM -1: **charla** *f.* (from the verb *charlar* meaning "to chat").

SYNONYM -2: **movida** *f. (Spain).*

trupe *f.* group of friends or family members, (the whole) gang.

example: Me encanta ir de vacaciones con toda la **trupe**.

translation: I love going on vacation with the whole **gang**.

SYNONYM -1: **ganga** *f. (Puerto Rico)* applies to a whole family or group of friends.

SYNONYM -2: **peña** *f. (Spain).*

Practice the Vocabulary

(*Answers to Lesson 5, p. 177*)

A. Complete the phrases by choosing the appropriate word(s) from the list below. Make any necessary changes.

adoquín	**comer(se) el coco**	**merengue**
arreglar(se)	**contado**	**mugre**
chulada	**escuincle**	**tertulia**
comecocos	**Hombre**	**trupe**

1. Marta está preciosa cuando se ________________ .
2. Alejandro siempre está haciendo tonterías. Es un ______________ .
3. No se como me manché mi camisa pero está llena de __________ .
4. ¡________________! Me alegro de verte.
5. ¡Vamos al gran alcacén con toda la ________________ !
6. Mario es un ________________. Cree que su opinión es la única que cuenta.
7. ¡Esa motocicleta es una ________________ !
8. Mira cuantos ________________ hay en el parque hoy.
9. No intentes ________________ porque no te voy a hacer caso de todas maneras.
10. Esa mujer es preciosa. ¡Es un verdadero ________________ !
11. Voy a comprarlos ahora y voy a paga al ______________.
12. Todos los viernes por la noche tenemos ________________ en casa de Juan.

B. Underline the word(s) that best complete(s) the phrase.

1. Antonio es un (**bebecocos**, **tomacocos**, **comecocos**). Siempre cree tener la razón.

2. ¡(**Hombre**, **Caballero**, **Señor**)! ¡Claro que me gustan los pasteles!

3. Te ves muy guapa cuando te (**arriendas**, **arreglas**, **arrestan**).

4. ¡Esta casa es una (**chopada**, **chulada**, **chuleta**)!

5. Felipe es un (**ladrillo**, **adoquín**, **albardán**). Nunca hace nada bien.

6. No me gusta nada esta obra de teatro. Es muy (**chunga**, **chispa**, **chota**).

7. No te comas el (**coco**, **melón**, **pato**). No es para tanto.

8. Mañana voy de vacaciones a Florida con toda la (**tripa**, **trupe**, **tropa**).

9. Esta noche tenemos (**tertulia**, **tarántula**, **trueque**) en casa de Ramón.

10. Parece que nunca lava su auto. Mira cuánta (**mútula**, **mugre**, **murria**) tiene.

11. Siempre me gusta pagar (**al contar**, **al cantar**, **al contado**).

12. ¡Mira cuántos (**escuincles**, **esculapios**, **erizos**) hay en la heladería de la esquina.

C. Match the Spanish with the English translation by writing the corresponding letter of the answer in the box.

☐ 1. For crying outloud! Of course I love you!

☐ 2. I love going shopping with the whole gang.

☐ 3. Look at Maria! She's such a babe!

☐ 4. I always pay cash when I go shopping.

☐ 5. I didn't know you had three kids!

☐ 6. I love it when you fix yourself up.

☐ 7. Please don't get all worked up about it.

☐ 8. This boat is so cool!

☐ 9. What a bad film!

☐ 10. Julio is such a jerk.

☐ 11. Luis's house is so dirty.

☐ 12. We're going to have a get-together tonight.

A. **Vamos a tener una tertulia esta noche.**

B. **Julio es un adoquín.**

C. **La casa de Luis está llena de mugre.**

D. **¡Hombre! ¡Claro que te quiero!**

E. **¡Este barco es una chulada!**

F. **Me encanta ir de compras con toda la trupe.**

G. **Siempre pago al contado cuando voy de compras.**

H. **¡Yo no sabía que tenías tres escuincles!**

I. **Por favor, no te comas el coco.**

J. **¡Qué película más chunga!**

K. **Me encanta cuando te arreglas.**

L. **¡Mira María! ¡Es un verdadero merengue!**

D. Complete the dialogue using the list below.

adoquín	**comecocos**	**merengue**
arreglas	**contado**	**mugre**
chulada	**escuincle**	**tertulia**
coco	**Hombre**	**trupe**

Esperanza: ¡__________________! Cuando te __________________ te ves bellísima. Los chicos van a pensar que eres un verdadero __________________ cuando te vean en la __________ de esta noche. Espero que no creas que soy un ____________ , pero ese vestido es una __________________. Es mucho más bonito que el vestido que te pusiste antes. Parecías un __________________ .

Irene: Tienes razón. Pero este me encanta. De hecho, creo que también voy a comprar el bolso y los zapatos que van con este vestido. No quiero venir con toda la ______________ , así que voy a comprarlos ahora y voy a pagar al __________ . Espero que no se me ensucie. La última vez que me puse algo caro para ir a una fiesta, un ________________ derramó comida encima mía.

Esperanza: No te comas el ____________________ tanto. Además, si ves que tiene un poquito de ____________________ , lo puedes lavar.

E. DICTATION
Test Your Aural Comprehension

(This dictation can be found in the Appendix on page 191.)

If you are following along with your cassette, you will now hear a series of sentences from the opening dialogue. These sentences will be read by a native speaker at normal conversational speed (which may seem fast to you at first). In addition, the words will be pronounced *as you would actually hear them in a conversation,* oftentimes including some common reductions.

The first time the sentences are presented, simply listen in order to get accustomed to the speed and heavy use of reductions. The sentences will then be read again with a pause after each to give you time to write down what you heard. The third time the sentences are read, follow along with what you have written.

REVIEW EXAM FOR LESSONS 1-5

(*Answers to Review, p. 178*)

A. Underline the correct definition of the word(s) in boldface.

1. **chocante**:
   a. annoying — b. nice
2. **chulear**:
   a. to work — b. to act cool
3. **donnadie**:
   a. important person — b. loser
4. **enano**:
   a. tall person — b. short person
5. **platicar**:
   a. to sing — b. to talk
6. **bocaza**:
   a. large nose — b. big mouth
7. **cruda**:
   a. hangover — b. toothache
8. **cachas**:
   a. beautiful woman — b. good-looking guy
9. **besugo**:
   a. idiot — b. smart person
10. **currar**:
    a. to work — b. to run
11. **poli**:
    a. polite person — b. police

12. **talego**:
    a. hotel b. jail

13. **casinadie**:
    a. very important person b. a nobody

14. **chusma**:
    a. jet set b. despicable person

15. **chupar**:
    a. to drink b. to sing

16. **colarse**:
    a. to cut in line b. to collect

17. **cuadrado (estar)**:
    a. to be skinny b. to be muscular

18. **empollón**:
    a. nerd b. hunk

19. **pachanga**:
    a. funeral b. party

20. **trastornado (estar)**:
    a. to be furious b. to be happy

21. **buitre**:
    a. big spender b. cheapskate

22. **rechulo**:
    a. ugly b. cool

23. **escuincle**:
    a. small child b. old person

B. Complete the following phrases by choosing the appropriate word(s) from the list below.

adoquín	**chelas**	**colmo**
ascuas	**chismear**	**suertudo**
buenona	**chollo**	**tertulia**
chambear	**chulada**	**trupe**

1. ¡Esto es el ________________ !

2. El auto de Jorge es una verdadera ________________ .

3. Hoy tuve que ________________ dos horas extras.

4. ¡Qué ________________ soy! ¡Me tocó la lotería!

5. Pedro está en ________________ . Parece que le va a dar un ataque de nervios.

6. Mira que cuerpo tiene Yolanda. ¡Es una verdadera ____________ !

7. Mañana vamos a ir a la playa con toda la ________________ .

8. Este hotel es un ________________ . Es muy barato y muy bueno.

9. Manuel es un ________________ . No sabe ni escribir.

10. ¿Quieres ir a tomar unas ________________ al bar de la esquina?

11. Esta noche vamos a ir a una ________________ en casa de Luis.

12. A Pablo le encanta ______________ sobre Anabel.

C. Match the Spanish with the English translation by writing the corresponding letter of the answer in the box.

☐ 1. Alejandro loves to show off his car.

☐ 2. That guy is such a loser.

☐ 3. Manuel is such a pain in the neck.

☐ 4. My mother loves to talk up a storm.

☐ 5. I don't feel well. I have a hangover.

☐ 6. One of these days, Luis is going to end up in jail.

☐ 7. Miguel is on pins and needles waiting to see if he's going to get his promotion.

☐ 8. I hate working at the supermarket.

☐ 9. My parents live in Los Angeles.

☐ 10. Okay! I'll go with you.

☐ 11. For crying outlod! Of course I like to eat seafood.

☐ 12. Look at Rosalinda! She's such a babe.

A. **Ese tipo es un donnadie.**

B. **A mi madre le encanta enrollarse mucho.**

C. **¡Hombre! Claro que me gusta comer mariscos.**

D. **Miguel está en ascuas porque está esperando si le van a dar su promoción.**

E. **Odio chambear en el supermercado.**

F. **Mis viejos viven in Los Angeles.**

G. **A Alejandro le encanta chulear de coche.**

H. **¡Mira Rosalinda! Es una verdadera buenona.**

I. **¡Vale! Iré contigo.**

J. **Uno de estos días, Luis va a acabar en el talego.**

K. **No me siento bien. Tengo una cruda.**

L. **Manuel es un latón.**

D. Underline the appropriate word that best completes the phrase.

1. ¡(**Caramba**, **Carambola**, **Cachis**)! ¡Qué calor hace!

2. Ese tipo es un (**nadie**, **señornadie**, **donnadie**). No tiene trabajo y además no tiene intención de encontrar uno.

3. Mi maestro de literatura es un (**enano**, **elébora**, **elegido**). Ni siquiera alcanza el pizarrón.

4. ¡Mira la (**bocura**, **bocaza**, **boquera**) que tiene Julio!

5. Esta noche vamos a pasarlo bien en una (**pachanga**, **pachera**, **papata**).

6. Sergio es muy guapo. Es un verdadero (**cachito**, **cachos**, **cachas**).

7. Esa mujer come demasiado. Es una (**foco**, **foquero**, **foca**).

8. Parece que Miguel tiene mucha (**lana**, **plana**, **llana**). Siempre usa ropa cara.

9. ¡Mi hermano se llevó mi coche sin mi permiso otra vez! ¡Esto es el (**calma**, **colmo**, **colmura**)!

10. Hoy estoy (**amuermado**, **amuermatado**, **amuertado**). Creo que necesito dormir un poco.

11. Mis (**viejos**, **nuevos**, **viejudos**) se fueron de vacaciones.

12. Felipe es un (**comenaranjas**, **comecocos**, **cocudo**). ¡Ojalá se guardara su opinión para sí mismo!

LECCIÓN SEIS

Parece que mi nueva vecina tiene una *caradura* increíble.

(trans.): My new neighbor seems like a real ***arrogant person****.*
(lit.): My new neighbor seems like an incredible ***hard-face****.*

Lección Seis

Dialogue in Slang

Parece que mi nueva vecina tiene una caradura increíble.

Susana: Hoy **conocí** a los nuevos vecinos. Como soy un **manitas**, fui a ver si necesitaban ayuda. Pero me dieron un **corte**, porque me dijeron que no. Son tan **raros** que **me largué** en seguida.

Cuquita: No parece que sean muy simpáticos. ¿Cómo son de aspecto físico?

Susana: Bueno, ella es una **carroza** y además parece que tiene una **caradura** increíble. A lo mejor hace unos años era un **caramelo** pero ahora es verdaderamente **horripilante**. Y él es tan **pesado**. Es un **cuatrojos** con el **coco** muy pequeño y unas **antenas** gigantes. ¡Que parejita! Y deberías de haber visto su casa. Había un **cochazo** en el garaje y una **pila** de juguetes en el jardín. Me da la impresíon de que tienen un **montón** de **renacuajos**.

Cuquita: ¡Parece que están **a flote**!

Lesson Six

Susana: Today I **met** the new neighbors. Since I'm such a **handyman**, I went over to see if they could use any help. But they **cut me off** and just said no. They were so **weird**, I couldn't wait **to leave**.

Cuquita: They don't sound very friendly. What did they look like?

Susana: Well, she's an **old relic** and besides she seemed incredibly **arrogant**. Years ago she must have been a total **fox** but now she's **horrifying**. And he seems like such a **pain in the neck**. He **wears glasses** and has a small **head** with gigantic **ears**. What a pair, these two! And you should have seen their house. There was a **great car** in the garage and a **pile** of toys in the yard. I have the feeling that they have a **bunch** of **kids**.

Cuquita: They sound like they must be **well off**!

Vocabulary

antenas *f.pl. (Spain)* • (lit.): antennas.

example: Manolo tiene las **antenas** tan grandes que parece un elefante.

translation: Manolo has such **big ears** he looks like an elephant.

NOTE: **orejudo/a** *adj.* big-eared (from the feminine noun *oreja* meaning "ear").

SYNONYM: **guatacas** *f.pl. (Cuba).*

caradura *f.* • **1.** arrogant • **2.** nervy, brazen • (lit.): hard face.

example (1): Pedro es un **caradura**. Se cree que es mejor que nadie.

translation: Pedro is so **arrogant**. He thinks he's better than anybody else.

example (2): Jose Luis es tan **caradura** que siempre le pide dinero a sus amigos.

translation: Jose Luis is so **nervy**. He's always asking his friends for money.

SYNONYM: **descarado/a** *adj.* • (lit.): faceless (from the feminine noun *cara* meaning "face").

caramelo *m.* beautiful woman, knockout, "fox" • (lit.): candy.

example: Anabel es un verdadero **caramelo**. Se nota que se cuida.

translation: Anabel is a real **fox**. You can tell she takes care of herself.

SYNONYMS: SEE - **merengue**, *p. 72.*

carroza *f.* elderly person, old relic • (lit.): carriage.

example: Esa mujer es una **carroza**. Parece que tiene noventa años.

translation: That woman is an **old relic**. She looks like she is ninety.

SYNONYM -1: **abuelo** *m.* • (lit.): grandfather.

SYNONYM -2: **añoso** *m.* • (lit.): from the masculine noun *año* meaning "year."

SYNONYM -3: **antañón** *m.* • (lit.): from the masculine noun *antaño* meaning "long ago."

SYNONYM -4: **Más viejo que Matusalén** *exp.* very old person • (lit.): older than Methuselah.

SYNONYM -5: **prehistórico** *m.* • (lit.): prehistoric.

SYNONYM -6: **reliquia histórica** *f. (Cuba)* • (lit.): historic relic.

SYNONYM -7: **vejestorio** *m.* • (lit.): from the adjective *viejo* meaning "old."

SYNONYM -8: **vejete** *m.* • (lit.): from the adjective *viejo* meaning "old."

cochazo *m.* great car.

example: Alvaro tiene un **cochazo**. No sé cómo se puede permitir ese lujo.

translation: Alvaro has a **great car**. I don't know how he can afford it.

SYNONYMS: SEE - **bólido**, *p. 105*.

coco *m.* head • (lit.): coconut.

example: ¡Caramba! ¡Ese tipo tiene el **coco** enorme!

translation: Geez! That guy has a huge **head**!

SYNONYM -1: **azotea** *f. (Spain)* • (lit.): flat roof, terraced roof.

SYNONYM -2: **bocho** *m. (Argentina)*.

SYNONYM -3: **cachola** *f.* • (lit.): hounds.

SYNONYM -4: **cholla** *f.* • (lit.): mind, brain.

SYNONYM -5: **coco** *m.* • (lit.): coconut.

SYNONYM -6: **cráneo** *m.* • (lit.): cranium, skull.

SYNONYM -7: **mate** *m. (Argentina).*

SYNONYM -8: **melón** *m. (Argentina).*

SYNONYM -9: **molondra** *f.*

SYNONYM -10: **sesera** *f.* • (lit.): from the masculine noun *seso* meaning "brain."

SYNONYM -11: **terraza** *f. (Argentina).*

SYNONYM -12: **testa** *f.* • (lit.): from the Latin term *testa* meaning "head."

ALSO: **tener seco el coco** *exp.* to be / to go crazy • (lit.): to have the dried coconut.

VARIATION: **secársele a uno el coco** *exp.* • (lit.): to be in the process of getting one's coconut dried.

conocer [a alguien] *exp.* • **1.** to meet (NOTE: This usage of *conocer* is extremely popular throughout the Spanish-speaking communities • **2.** to be acquainted [with someone].

example: Ayer **conocí** a mis nuevos vecinos. Parecen muy buena gente.

translation: Yesterday I **met** my new neighbors. They seem to be good people.

ALSO -1: **conocer alguien de nombre** *exp.* to know someone by name.

ALSO -2: **conocer alguien de vista** *exp.* to know someone by sight.

corte (dar un) *exp.* to cut someone off, to answer someone back in an aggressive way • (lit.): to cut.

example: Quise ayudar a Ismael pero me **dió un corte** y me dijo no, gracias.

translation: I wanted to help Ismael but he **cut me off** and said no thank you.

ALSO: **¡Qué corte!** *exp.* • **1.** What a disappointment! • **2.** How embarrassing!

NOTE: Interestingly enough, simply by removing the indefinite article *un* from the expression *dar un corte,* another popular expression is created: **dar corte** *exp.* to be ashamed or embarrassed.

SYNONYM -1: **cortarón (dar un)** *exp. (Argentina).*

SYNONYM -2: **corte pastelillo (dar un)** *exp. (Puerto Rico).*

NOTE: **pastelillo** *m.* • (lit.): a fried pastry that has been folded in half and cut.

cuatroojos *m.* a person who wears glasses, "four-eyes" • (lit.): four eyes.

example: Mi maestro de literatura es un **cuatroojos**.

translation: My literature teacher is **four-eyed**.

NOTE: Also spelled: *cuatrojos.*

SYNONYM -1: **bisco/a** *n. (Argentina).*

SYNONYM -2: **cegato/a** *adj.* • (lit.): from the masculine noun *ciego* meaning "blind person."

SYNONYM -3: **chicato/a** *adj. (Argentina).*

SYNONYM -4: **corto de vista** *exp.* nearsighted • (lit.): shortsighted.

SYNONYM -5: **gafitas** *adj.* • (lit.): from the masculine noun *gafas* meaning "glasses."

SYNONYM -6: **gafudo/a** *adj.* • (lit.): from the masculine noun *gafas* meaning "glasses."

flote (estar a) *exp.* to be well off (monetarily).

example: Parece que Pedro está **a flote**. ¿Viste qué cochazo tiene?

translation: It seems like Pedro is **well off**. Did you see what a great car he drives?

SEE: **lana**, *p. 39.*

horripilante *adj.* horrifying, terrifying.

example: Esa película es **horripilante**. Me tuve que salir del cine.

translation: That's a **horrifying** movie. I had to get out of the theater.

SYNONYM -1: **espeluznante** *adj.* • (lit.): horrifying.

SYNONYM -2: **horroroso** *adj.* • (lit.): horrible, dreadful, hideous.

SYNONYM -3: **pavorosa** *adj.* • (lit.): frightful, terrifying.

largarse *v.* to leave, to go away, to beat it.

example: Como no me gustó el concierto, me **largué** en seguida.

translation: Since I didn't like the concert, I **left** after only a little while.

SYNONYM -1: **escabullirse** *v.* • (lit.): to slip (from, through, or out), to escape.

SYNONYM -2: **escurrirse** *v.* • (lit.): to drain, to slide.

SYNONYM -3: **evaporarse** *v.* • (lit.): to evaporate oneself.

SYNONYM -4: **marcharse** *v.* • (lit.): to go away, to leave.

manitas *m.* handyman • (lit.): little hands.

example: Pepe arregla todo en su casa. ¡Es un verdadero **manitas**!

translation: Pepe fixes everything in his house himself. He's a real **handyman**!

SYNONYM: **arreglatodo** *m.* (said of a man or woman) • (lit.): a fix-everything.

ANTONYM -1: **chambón** *adj.* • (lit.): awkward.

ANTONYM -2: **desmañado/a** *adj.* • (lit.): clumsy or awkward person.

ANTONYM -3: **incapaz** *adj.* • (lit.): incapable, unable.

ANTONYM -4: **patoso/a** *adj.* • (lit.): boring, dull.

ANTONYM -5: **torpe** *adj.* clumsy

ANTONYM -6: **zopenco/a** *adj.*

montón *m.* a bunch of, a lot of • (lit.): crowd.

example: Alfonso tiene un **montón** de amigos en todas partes porque es muy simpático.

translation: Alfonso has **a lot of** friends everywhere because he's very nice.

NOTE -1: **a montones** *exp.* in large quantities, abundantly • *libros a montones;* a large quantity of books (literally, "a mountain of books").

NOTE -2: **ser del montón** *exp.* to be mediocre • (lit.): to be of the crowd.

SYNONYM: **pila** *f.* • (lit.): a pile – see below.

pesado/a *adj.* dull, tiresome, annoying, irritating, pain in the neck • (lit.): heavy, massive, weighty.

example: Darío es un **pesado**. Siempre está contando historias aburridas.

translation: Dario is such a **pain in the neck**. He is always telling boring stories.

SYNONYM -1: **cargante** *adj.* • (lit.): loaded.

SYNONYM -2: **latoso/a** *adj.*

NOTE: This comes from the expression *dar la lata,* (literally meaning "to give the tin can," is used to mean "to annoy the living daylights out of someone").

ANTONYM: **chunguero** *adj.*

NOTE: This comes from the term *chunga* meaning "joke" or "jest."

pila *f.* a bunch of, a lot of, a pile of • (lit.): sink, basin.

example: Estoy muy ocupado. Tengo una **pila** de cosas que hacer.

translation: I'm very busy. I have **a bunch of** things to do.

SYNONYM: **montón** *m.* • (lit.): crowd – see above.

raro/a *adj.* weird, strange, peculiar • (lit.): rare.

example: Los Gonzalez son muy **raros**. Nunca salen de su casa.

translation: The Gonzalez's are very **weird**. They never leave their house.

ALSO: **rara vez** *exp.* seldom • (lit.): rare time.

SYNONYM: **lunático/a** *adj. & n.* • (lit.): lunatic.

renacuajo/a *n.* little kid, small child, shrimp, little runt • (lit.): tadpole.

example: En la casa de Manuel siempre hay un montón de **renacuajos**.

translation: There's always a lot of **small kids** at Manuel's house.

SYNONYM -1: **chiquillo/a** *n.*

NOTE: This noun comes from the adjective *chico/a* meaning "small."

SYNONYM -2: **chiquitín/a** *n.*

NOTE: This noun comes from the adjective *chico/a* meaning "small."

SYNONYM -3: **crío/a** *m.* • (lit.): a nursing-baby.

SYNONYM -4: **escuincle** *m.* little kid, small child.

SYNONYM -5: **gurrumino/a** *n.* • (lit.): weak or sickly person, "whimp."

SYNONYM -6: **mocoso/a** *n.* • (lit.): snotty-nosed person.

SYNONYM -7: **párvulo** *m.* • (lit.): tot.

SYNONYM -8: **pequeñajo/a** *n.*

NOTE: This noun comes from the adjective *pequeño/a* meaning "small."

SYNONYM -9: **pituso/a** *n.* smurf (from the cartoon characters).

ANTONYM -1: **grandote** *m.*

NOTE: This noun comes from the adjective *grande* meaning "big."

ANTONYM -2: **grandullón/a** *n.* big kid.

NOTE: This noun comes from the adjective *grande* meaning "big."

Practice the Vocabulary

(Answers to Lesson 6, p. 179)

A. Complete the following phrase by choosing the appropriate word from the list below.

antenas	**horripilante**
carroza	**manitas**
coco	**montón**
corte	**pesado**
cuatroojos	**raro**
flote	**renacuajo**

1. Pedro lo arregla todo. Es un verdadero ________________ .
2. Lynda es millonaria. Tiene un ________________ de dinero.
3. Luis nunca habla con nadie. Es muy ________________ .
4. ¡Mira qué ________________ tan grandes tiene este tipo!
5. Ese hombre es una ________________ . Parece que tiene cien años.
6. Hoy no me siento bien. Tengo dolor de ________________ .
7. Juan habla demasiado. Es un ________________ .
8. Fui a ver si necesitaban ayuda, pero me dieron un ________________ porque me dijeron que no.
9. Esa gente tiene una casa enorme. Parece que están a ____________ .
10. Ese policía ________________ me dio una multa.
11. Esa obra de teatro es ________________ . No me gustó nada.
12. Alfonso y Lynda tienen dos ________________ . Un niño de dos años y una niña de cinco.

B. Underline the word in parentheses that best completes the sentence.

1. Jorge es un (**carablanda**, **caricatura**, **caradura**). Siempre quiere que le invite.

2. Ana es preciosa. Es un verdadero (**caramelo**, **chocolate**, **chocolatina**).

3. ¡Mira que (**cacho**, **carra**, **cochazo**) tiene Agustín! Es un Corvette.

4. Ayer (**supe**, **sabía**, **conocí**) a mis nuevos vecinos. Son muy simpáticos.

5. No me gusta esta fiesta. Quiero (**largarme**, **plasmarme**, **arreglarme**) en seguida.

6. No tengo tiempo para nada. Tengo una (**batería**, **pila**, **polo**) de cosas que hacer.

7. Federico es un (**manitas**, **manotas**, **manutas**). Lo arregla todo.

8. Esa película es (**horripilante**, **cómico**, **terífico**). Me tuve que salir del cine.

9. Inés es muy popular. Tiene un (**manta**, **minuta**, **montón**) de amigos.

10. Gustavo es un (**renacuajo**, **sapo**, **rana**). Solo tiene dos años.

11. Mi profesor de matemáticas es un (**sieteojos**, **tresojos**, **cuatroojos**). ¡Me alegro que no tengo que usar gafas!

12. Ese tipo no tiene amigos. Es muy (**rarón**, **raro**, **rana**).

C. Match the Spanish with the English translation by writing the corresponding letter of the answer in the box.

☐ 1. Look what big ears that guy has!

☐ 2. Maria is an old relic.

☐ 3. Sara is a real fox.

☐ 4. Antonio has a great car.

☐ 5. Yesterday I met my girlfriend's parents.

☐ 6. I think he is well off.

☐ 7. Javier has a lot of friends.

☐ 8. I left the party after a little while.

☐ 9. Juan is a real handyman.

☐ 10. Lynda has two little kids.

☐ 11. Those two are very weird.

☐ 12. Marta is such a pain in the neck.

A. **Marta es una pesada.**

B. **Lynda tiene dos renacuajos.**

C. **Ayer conocí a los padres de mi novia.**

D. **¡Mira qué antenas más grandes tiene ese tipo!**

E. **Sara es un verdadero caramelo.**

F. **María es una carroza.**

G. **Creo que él está a flote.**

H. **Esos dos son muy raros.**

I. **Antonio tiene un cochazo.**

J. **Juan es un verdadero manitas.**

K. **Javier tiene un montón de amigos.**

L. **Me largué de la fiesta después de un ratito.**

D. CROSSWORD

Fill in the crossword puzzle on the opposite page by choosing the correct words from the list below.

antenas	**conocer**	**manitas**
caradura	**corte**	**montón**
caramelo	**cuatroojos**	**pesado**
carroza	**flote**	**pila**
cochazo	**horripilante**	**raro**
coco	**largarse**	**renacuajo**

ACROSS

1. ______ **(dar un)** *exp.* to cut someone off, to answer someone back in an aggressive way • (lit.): to cut.

16. ______ *adj.* horrifying, terrifying.

23. ______ *m.* head • (lit.): coconut.

28. ______ *m.* beautiful woman, knockout, "fox" • (lit.): candy.

32. ______ **[a alguien]** *exp.* • **1.** to meet • **2.** to be acquainted [with someone].

42. ______ *f.* a bunch of, a lot of, a pile of • (lit.): sink, basin.

43. ______ *v.* to leave, to go away, to beat it.

53. ______ *m.* a bunch of, a lot of • (lit.): crowd.

DOWN

1. ______ *m.* great car.

5. ______ *m.* handyman.

9. ______ *f.pl.* • (lit.): antennas.

12. ______ *m.* a person who wears glasses, "four-eyes."

17. ______ *n.* little kid, shrimp, little runt • (lit.): tadpole.

25. ______ *adj.* weird, strange, peculiar • (lit.): rare.

32. ______ *f.* • **1.** arrogant • **2.** nervy, brazen.

33. ______ *f.* elderly person, old relic • (lit.): carriage.

38. __________ **(estar a)** *exp.* to be well off (monetarily).

42. __________ *adj.* dull, tiresome, annoying, • (lit.): heavy, massive, weighty.

CROSSWORD PUZZLE

E. DICTATION
Test Your Aural Comprehension

(This dictation can be found in the Appendix on page 191.)

If you are following along with your cassette, you will now hear a series of sentences from the opening dialogue. These sentences will be read by a native speaker at normal conversational speed (which may seem fast to you at first). In addition, the words will be pronounced *as you would actually hear them in a conversation,* oftentimes including some common reductions.

The first time the sentences are presented, simply listen in order to get accustomed to the speed and heavy use of reductions. The sentences will then be read again with a pause after each to give you time to write down what you heard. The third time the sentences are read, follow along with what you have written.

LECCIÓN SIETE

Mira ese jugador *narizón*. ¡Qué *ardilla*!

(trans.): *Look at that guy with the **big honker**. What a **smart cookie**!*

(lit.): *Look at that **big-nosed** player. What a **squirrel**!*

Lección Siete

Dialogue in Slang

Mira ese jugador narizón. ¡Qué ardilla!

Carlos: ¡**Vaya**!, ¡mi **amiguete**! ¿Qué haces aquí?

Alfredo: Voy a **verme con** Julio, pero nunca **aparece a tiempo**. Su **bólido** siempre tiene alguna avería. Es un verdadero **cacharro**. ¿Qué hora es?

Carlos: Ahora **son como** las dos de la tarde y el partido va a empezar muy pronto. Creo que va a ser un buen partido porque juega Juan Vázquez.

Alfredo: ¿Te refieres al jugador **narizón**? ¿El que **se da lija**? Yo siempre pensé que el juega **malísimamente**. Es un **chupón**. Le gusta **regatear** demasiado y nunca le da al balón.

Carlos: ¡**Qué va**! Yo creo que ese tío es una **ardilla**. Lo que pasa es que quiere que el otro equipo se crea que no sabe jugar y en el último momento siempre **mete un gol**. **Se menea** mejor que nadie.

Alfredo: Bueno, entonces es un buen **bailón**, pero un jugador muy **chungo**.

Carlos: ¡Espero que estés **vacilando**!

Lesson Seven

Carlos: **Hey**, **pal**! What are you doing here?

Alfredo: I'm going **to meet** Julio, but he never **shows up on time**. His **car** is always breaking down. It's a real **lemon**. What time is it?

Carlos: It's **about** 2:00pm and the game is going to begin soon. It should be a great game because Juan Vázquez is playing.

Alfredo: You mean the player **with the huge nose**? The one **with the attitude problem**? I always thought he played **really badly**. He **hogs the ball**. He likes **to shuffle** it around too much and he always misses the ball.

Carlos: **Get outta here**! I think the guy's a **smart cookie**. He just wants the other team to think he can't play, then at the last minute, he **scores a goal**. He **moves** better than anyone.

Alfredo: Great. Then he's a good **dancer**, just a **lousy** player.

Carlos: I can only hope you're **joking**!

Vocabulary

amiguete *m. (Spain)* pal, buddy, friend.

example: Felipe es mi **amiguete**. Siempre puedo contar con él.

translation: Felipe is my **pal**. I can always count on him.

VARIATION: **amigote** *m.*

NOTE: **amiguete del alma** *exp.* bosom buddy, close friend • (lit.): buddy of the soul.

SYNONYM -1: **colega** *m. (Spain)* • (lit.): colleague.

SYNONYM -2: **cuate** *m. (Mexico)* pal, buddy.

SYNONYM -3: **tronco** *m. (Argentina)* • (lit.): truck (of a tree).

aparecer a tiempo *exp.* to arrive on time • to appear on time.

example: Mi maestro de matemáticas siempre **aparece a tiempo**.

translation: My math teacher always **shows up on time**.

SYNONYM: **llagar a tiempo** *exp.* • (lit.): to arrive on time.

ardilla *adj.* smart, bright, sharp • (lit.): squirrel.

example: Linda sabe mucho de computadoras. Es una verdadera **ardilla**.

translation: Linda knows a lot about computers. She's really **bright**.

SYNONYM -1: **águila** *m. (Cuba)* • (lit.): eagle.

SYNONYM -2: **listillo/a** *adj. (Spain).*

NOTE: This comes from the adjective *listo* meaning "clear" or "smart."

SYNONYM -3: **piola** *f. (Argentina)* a smart and clever person.

SYNONYM -4: **zorra** *f. (Puerto Rico)* • (lit.): fox.

ANTONYM: **burro/a** *adj.* dumb, stupid • (lit.): donkey – SEE: *p. 120*.

bailón *m. (Spain)* dancer (usually applies to a Spanish folk dancer).

example: Andrés conoce a muchas chicas porque es un gran **bailón** y siempre va a las discotecas.

translation: Andrés knows a lot of girls because he's a great **dancer** and goes to discos al the time.

NOTE: This comes from the verb *bailar* meaning "to dance."

SYNONYM: **bailador/a** *n. (Spain).*

bólido *m. (Spain)* car, automobile • (lit.): race car.

example: Ana y yo vamos a dar una vuelta en mi **bólido** nuevo.

translation: Ana and I are going for a ride in my new **car**.

NOTE: In formal Spanish, this term usually refers to a great car, although it occasionally used in a sarcastic way referring to a car that does not work properly.

SYNONYM -1: **autazo** *m. (Argentina).*

SYNONYM -2: **auto** *m. (Argentina).*

SYNONYM -3: **buga** *f. (Spain).*

SYNONYM -4: **carrazo** *m. (Puerto Rico / Cuba)* big car.

SYNONYM -5: **cochazo** *m.*

SYNONYM -6: **coche** *m. (Argentina).*

SYNONYM -7: **carro** *m. (Mexico / Cuba).*

SYNONYM -8: **máquina** *f. (Puerto Rico)* machine.

cacharro *m.* • **1.** jalopy, old wreck • **2.** lemon (any piece of machinery that does not work properly).

example (1): Este **cacharro** nunca quiere arrancar por las mañanas.

translation: This **old wreck** never wants to start in the morning.

example (2): Este lavaplatos no limpia los platos bien. Es un **cacharro**.

translation: This dishwasher doesn't clean the dishes properly. It's a **piece of junk**.

SYNONYM: **porquería** *f. (Argentina)* said of anything worthless.

chungo/a *adj.* "uncool," lousy, ugly.

example: Esa película es muy **chunga**. Cuando fui a verla me quedé dormido.

translation: That's a really **lousy** movie. When I went to see it I fell asleep.

SYNONYM -1: **chango/a** *adj. (Puerto Rico).*

SYNONYM -2: **flojo/a** *adj. (Mexico / Puerto Rico).*

ANTONYM: **chulo/a** *adj.* cool, neat, great, good-looking.

chupón *m.* a player who tends to hog the ball.

example: Ernesto es un **chupón**. Nunca pasa la pelota a los demás jugadores.

translation: Ernesto **hogs the ball**. He never passes the ball to the rest of the players.

NOTE: This term is used mostly in soccer games.

SYNONYM: **peleón** *m. (Puerto Rico)* one who plays like the famous soccer player, Pele.

como (ser) *exp.* (referring to time) approximately, about • (lit.): to be like.

example: Tengo mucho sueño. ¡Ya **son como** las dos de la madrugada!

translation: I'm very sleepy. It's **about** two o'clock in the morning!

darse lija *exp.* to put on airs, to act pretentious, to have an attitude problem • (lit.): to give oneself sandpaper.

example: A Ricardo le gusta **darse lija**. Cree que es mejor que nadie.

translation: Ricardo likes to **put on airs**. He thinks he's better than anybody else.

SYNONYM: **ser un broncas** *adj. (Spain)* to have a bad attitude, said of someone who is always in fights.

malísimamente *adv.* really badly, terribly (from the adverb *mal* meaning "poorly").

example: Juan jugó **malísimamente**.

translation: Juan played **really badly**.

SYNONYM -1: **de pena** *exp.* • (lit.): of shame.

SYNONYM -2: **pésimamente** *adv.* • (lit.): very badly, wretchedly.

ANTONYM: **buenísimamente** *adv.* (from the adverb *bueno* meaning "good") really well, fantastically.

menearse *v.* to move, dance.

example: Me encanta cómo **se menea** Alberto. Baila muy bien.

translation: I love how Alberto **moves**. He really dances well.

SYNONYM -1: **bailotear** *v.*

NOTE: This term comes from the verb *bailar* meaning "to dance."

SYNONYM -2: **moverse** *v.* • (lit.): to move.

ALSO: **mover la colita** *exp.* • (lit.): to move or shake one's tail.

NOTE: This expression comes from a popular Spanish song meaning "to shake one's booty."

meter un gol *exp.* to score a goal • (lit.): to put in a goal.

example: No me puedo creer que Luis **metió seis goles** en el partido de ayer.

translation: I can't believe Luis **scored six goals** in yesterday's game.

NOTE: This expression is used primarily in soccer games although it may also be used in similar sports such as hockey, waterpolo, etc.

narizón *adj.* big-nosed.

example: ¡Mira su **narizón**!

translation: Look at his **big nose**!

NOTE -1: This comes from the feminine noun *nariz* meaning "nose." In Spanish, special suffixes are commonly attached to nouns, adjectives, and adverbs to intensify their meaning. In this case, the suffix *zón* is added to the word *nariz*, transforming it to *narizón*, or "honker," "schnozzola," etc. To say "Look at his big nose!" in Spanish, it would certainly be more colloquial to say *¡Mira su **narizón**!* rather than *¡Mira su gran nariz!* The same would apply to other nouns as well, such as *cabeza*, meaning "head": *¡Mira su **cabezón**!* rather than *!Mira su gran cabeza!*

NOTE -2: When a noun is modified using the suffix *zón*, it may be used interchangeably as an adjective:

NOUN: *¡Mira su **nariz**!*
(Look at his nose!)

¡Mira su ***cabeza***!
(Look at his head!)

MODIFIED NOUN: ¡Mira su ***narizón***!
(Look at his big honker!)

¡Mira su **cabezón**!
(Look at his big head!)

MODIFIED ADJECTIVE: ¡Es un tipo ***narizón***!
(He's a big-nosed guy!)

¡Es un tipo ***cabezón***!
(He's a big-headed guy!)

VARIATION: **narigón** *adj.*

ANTONYM: **chato/a** *adj.* flat-nosed, pug-nosed.

¡Qué va! *exclam.* Baloney! No way! Get out of here! • (lit.): What goes!

example: ¿Tú crees que va a llover hoy?
!Qué va! ¿No ves que hace sol?

translation: Do you think it's going to rain today?
No way! Don't you see the sun is out?

SYNONYM -1: **¡Qué bobada!** *exclam.* What nonsense!

SYNONYM -2: **¡Qué disparate!** *exclam.* What baloney!

SYNONYM -3: **¡Qué tontería!** *exclam.* What stupidity!

NOTE: This exclamation is not used in Argentina or Uruguay.

regatear *v. (a popular soccer term)* to hoard • (lit.): to bargain.

example: Los otros jugadores odian a Maradona porque le gusta **regatear** mucho.

translation: The other players can't stand Maradona because he likes to **hoard** the ball a lot.

NOTE: This refers to the act of hoarding the ball in a soccer game.

SYNONYM: **chupar** *v.* • (lit.): to suck.

vacilar *v.* • **1.** to joke around, to clown around, to tease • **2.** to have a good time • **3.** to show off.

example (1): A Manuel le gusta **vacilar**.

translation: Manuel loves to **joke around**.

example (2): Me encanta **vacilar** con mis amigos los sábados por la noche.

translation: I love **having a good time** with my friends on Saturday nights.

example (3): Me gusta mucho **vacilar** con mi moto nueva.

translation: I love **showing off** my new motorcycle.

ALSO: **vacilón** *m.* • **1.** spree, party, shindig • **2.** something funny, cool, neat.

SYNONYM -1: **bromar** *v. (Spain)* (from the feminine noun *broma* meaning "joke").

SYNONYM -2: **chirigotear** *v.* to clown around.

SYNONYM -3: **pitorrearse** *v.* • **1.** to clown around • **2.** to make fun of someone.

¡Vaya! *interj.* • **1.** *(used to indicate surprise or amazement)* Well! How about that! • **2.** *(commonly used to modify a noun)* What an amazing... • **3.** *(used to modify a statement)* Really! • (lit.): Go!

example (1): ¡**Vaya**! Parece que va a empezar a llover.

translation: **How about that**! It looks like it's going to start raining.

example (2): ¡**Vaya** equipo! • !**Vaya** calor!

translation: **What a** team! • **What** heat!

example (3): Es un buen tipo, ¡**vaya**!

translation: What a good guy. **Really**!

SYNONYM -1: **¡Che!** *interj. (Argentina).*

SYNONYM -2: **¡Vamos!** *interj.* • (lit.): Let's go!

NOTE -1: *Vamos* may also be used within a sentence to indicate that the speaker has just changed his/her mind or is making a clarification. In this case, *vamos* is translated as "well."

example: Es guapa. **Vamos**, no es fea.

translation: She's pretty. **Well**, she's not ugly.

NOTE -2: Both *vaya* and *vamos* are extremely popular and both come from the verb *ir* meaning "to go."

verse con alguien *exp.* to meet someone • (lit.): to see oneself with someone.

example: Mañana me voy a **ver con** mi jefe. Espero que me aumente el sueldo.

translation: Tomorrow I'm going to **meet with** my boss. I hope he's going to raise my salary.

ALSO: **quedar con alguien** *exp.* to make an appointment with someone • (lit.): to remain with someone.

Practice the Vocabulary 

(Answers to Lesson 7, p. 181)

A. Underline the correct definition of the slang word(s) in boldface.

1. **ardilla**:
   a. smart — b. stupid

2. **cacharro**:
   a. new car — b. old jalopy

3. **amiguete**:
   a. pal — b. enemy

4. **darse lija**:
   a. to put on airs — b. to give something away

5. **meter un gol**:
   a. to miss a goal — b. to score a goal

6. **narizón**:
   a. short person — b. big-nosed person

7. **aparecer a tiempo**:
   a. to show up late — b. to show up on time

8. **vacilar**:
   a. to joke around — b. to be serious about something

9. **verse con alguien**:
   a. to look at someone — b. to meet someone

10. **¡Qué va!**:
    a. No way! — b. Of course!

11. **¡Vaya!**:
    a. How about that! — b. Let's go!

12. **menearse**:
    a. to stand still — b. to dance

B. Complete the sentences by choosing the appropriate word(s) from the list below. Make all necessary changes.

ardilla	**chupón**	**qué va**
bailón	**como (ser)**	**regatear**
bólido	**malísimamente**	**vacilar**
chungo	**narizón**	**ver(se)**

1. Ya es tarde. ____________________ las diez de la noche.

2. No me ha gustado la cena. He comido ____________________ .

3. Ese tipo es una verdadera ____________________ . Sabe más que nadie.

4. ¡____________________! Estás completamente equivocado.

5. Mañana me voy a ______________ con mi jefe. Espero que me aumente el sueldo.

6. ¡Mira el ____________________ que tiene ese tipo! Se parece a Pinocho.

7. ¿Te gusta mi nuevo ____________________ ? Lo acabo de comprar.

8. No estoy hablando en serio. Solamente estoy ____________________ .

9. Este hotel es muy ____________________ . Ni siquiera tiene baño en la habitación.

10. A ese futbolista le encanta ____________________ .

11. A Pedro le encanta ir a la discoteca. ¡Es un ____________________ !

12. No me gusta ese jugador porque es un ____________________ .

C. Match the Spanish with the English translation by writing the corresponding letter of the answer in the box.

☐ 1. That's a really lousy movie.

☐ 2. Do you want to go for a ride in my new car?

☐ 3. Pablo hogs the ball.

☐ 4. Javier likes to put on airs.

☐ 5. Look at his big honker!

☐ 6. I love how Patricia moves.

☐ 7. Sergio got to work at about 6 o'clock.

☐ 8. Estefanía is really smart.

☐ 9. Tomás is my pal.

☐ 10. What a team! They won every game they played.

☐ 11. No way! You're wrong!

☐ 12. Tomorrow I'm going to meet with Lynda.

A. **¡Qué va! ¡Estás equivocado!**

B. **Mañana voy a verme con Lynda.**

C. **¡Vaya equipo! Han ganado todos los partidos que han jugado.**

D. **Esa película es muy chunga.**

E. **Pablo es un chupón.**

F. **Tomás es mi amiguete.**

G. **A Javier le gusta darse lija.**

H. **¿Quieres ir a dar una vuelta en mi nuevo bólido?**

I. **Estefanía es una verdadera ardilla.**

J. **Sergio llegó al trabajo como a las seis.**

K. **¡Mira qué narizón!**

L. **Me encanta como se menea Patricia.**

D. WORD SEARCH

Circle the words in the grid on the next page that fit the following expressions. Words may be spelled up, down, or across.

regatear	**lija**	**vacilar**
bailón	**malísimamente**	**vaya**
chungo	**cacharro**	**chupón**
como	**menearse**	**verse**
gol	**narizón**	**amiguete**
ardilla	**tiempo**	**bólido**

1. ______________ *m.* pal, buddy, friend.
2. ______________ *adj.* smart, bright, sharp • (lit.): squirrel.
3. ______________ *m.* dancer.
4. ______________ *m.* car, automobile • (lit.): race car.
5. ______________ *m.* • **1.** jalopy, old wreck • **2.** lemon (any piece of machinery that does not work properly).
6. ______________ *adj.* "uncool," lousy, ugly.
7. ______________ *m.* a player who tends to hog the ball.
8. ______________ **ser** *exp.* (referring to time) approximately.
9. **darse** ______________ *exp.* to put on airs, to act pretentious, to have an attitude problem • (lit.): to give oneself sandpaper.
10. ________________________________ *adv.* really badly, terribly.
11. ______________ *v.* to move, dance.
12. **meter un** ______________ *exp.* to score a goal.
13. ______________ *adj.* big-nosed.
14. **aparecer a** ______________ *exp.* to arrive on time.
15. ______________ *v. (a popular soccer term)* to hoard • (lit.): to bargain.
16. ______________ *v.* • **1.** to joke around, to clown around • **2.** to have a good time • **3.** to show off.

17. ¡________________! *interj.* • **1.** *(used to indicate surprise)* well! how about that! • **2.** *(commonly used to modify a noun)* what an amazing... • **3.** *(used to modify a statement)* really! • (lit.): go.

18. ________________**con alguien** *exp.* to meet someone • (lit.): to see oneself with someone.

FIND-A-WORD PUZZLE

M	B	R	T	I	M	E	L	M	N	G	W
T	A	L	E	G	C	H	U	P	Ó	N	T
M	I	D	O	W	O	C	E	U	W	Z	R
A	L	A	L	A	M	H	M	R	A	P	A
B	Ó	L	I	D	O	U	U	T	I	A	S
C	N	A	J	A	A	F	R	I	L	V	T
U	E	O	A	M	I	G	U	E	T	E	O
V	M	L	A	A	T	M	O	M	Y	R	R
A	R	D	I	L	L	A	L	P	M	S	N
Y	R	C	T	Í	O	S	I	O	E	E	A
A	P	U	E	S	B	E	S	U	V	O	D
H	N	A	R	I	Z	Ó	N	O	A	R	O
U	C	N	R	M	Y	F	E	N	C	D	H
C	A	C	H	A	R	R	O	S	I	O	O
H	L	I	U	M	U	C	S	E	L	M	W
U	M	S	R	E	G	A	T	E	A	R	A
N	O	T	N	N	M	A	N	G	R	R	S
G	O	L	I	T	A	D	V	M	M	M	T
O	Y	M	M	E	N	E	A	R	S	E	A

E. DICTATION
Test Your Aural Comprehension

(This dictation can be found in the Appendix on page 192.)

If you are following along with your cassette, you will now hear a series of sentences from the opening dialogue. These sentences will be read by a native speaker at normal conversational speed (which may seem fast to you at first). In addition, the words will be pronounced *as you would actually hear them in a conversation,* oftentimes including some common reductions.

The first time the sentences are presented, simply listen in order to get accustomed to the speed and heavy use of reductions. The sentences will then be read again with a pause after each to give you time to write down what you heard. The third time the sentences are read, follow along with what you have written.

LECCIÓN OCHO

¡Qué *burro*!

(trans.): What a ***jerk****!*
(lit.): What a ***donkey****!*

Lección Ocho

Dialogue in Slang

¡Qué burro!

Anabel: ¿Cuando vamos a llegar? Yo no tenía ni idea que la feria estaba tan **allá**.

Marcelo: Quisiera poder **correr** más, pero lo que pasa es que hay muchos **domingueros** en la carretera. Ya sabes, la última vez que fui a la feria tardé seis horas porque me dieron un **regalito**...¡**se me pinchó una llanta**!

Anabel: ¡Qué **lata**!

Marcelo: ¡Creí que iba a **romper a** llorar! Yo creía que era lo bastante **vivo** como para cambiar la llanta, así que lo hice yo mismo. Pero mientras estaba cambiándola, me dieron un **leñazo** en la **azotea** porque un **burro** me tiró una lata de soda desde su bólido. ¡Qué **desmadre**! ¡Me enojé tanto!

Anabel: ¡Qué **rollo**! Bueno, yo no creo que tengas que preocuparte de eso esta vez porque ¡la feria está allí mismo!

Marcelo: ¡**Olé**! Espero que no haya desmasiados **chamacos**. El año pasado se **colaban** en todos los **cacharritos** más divertidos.

Lesson Eight

Anabel: When are we going to arrive? I had no idea the carnival was so **far away**.

Marcelo: I'd like **to drive** faster, but the problem is that there are so many **Sunday drivers** on the road. You know, the last time I went to the carnival, it took me six hours because I was given a **little surprise**...**I got a flat tire**!

Anabel: What a **pain in the butt**!

Marcelo: I thought I was going **to start** crying! I figured that I was **smart** enough to change a tire, so I did it myself. But when I was in the middle of changing it, I got **hit** in the **head** because some **jerk** threw a can of soda at me from his car. What a **mess**! I was so mad!

Anabel: What an **ordeal**! Well, I don't think you have to worry about that happening this time because the carnival is right here!

Marcelo: **Yippee**! I hope there aren't too many **kids** here. Last year they kept **cutting in line** at all the fun **rides**.

Vocabulary

allá (estar tan) *exp.* to be very far away • (lit.): to be so there.

example: ¡Yo no sabía que Chicago **estaba tan allá**!

translation: I didn't know Chicago was **so far away**!

ALSO: **muy allá** *exp.* very far away • (lit.): very there.

azotea *f.* head • (lit.): flat or terraced roof.

example: ¡Caramba! Parece que este tío está mal de la **azotea.**

translation: Geez! I think that guy is **crazy**.

SYNONYMS: SEE - **coco**, *p. 89*.

burro *m.* jerk, fool, moron, simpleton, stupid person • (lit.): donkey.

example: José es un **burro**. Nunca hace nada bien.

translation: Jose is a **moron**. He never does anything right.

SYNONYMS: SEE - **adoquín**, *p. 68*.

cacharritos *m.pl.* rides in an amusement park • (lit.): small pieces of junk, small machines that don't work properly.

example: Cuando fuimos al parque de atracciones David y Stefani se subieron en todos los **cacharritos**.

translation: When we went to the amusement park, David and Stefani went on every **ride**.

NOTE: This is a very popular expression especially among kids.

chamaco/a *n.* little kid, small child.

example: Esos **chamacos** pasan todo el día jugando en el parque.

translation: Those **kids** spend all day playing at the park.

SYNONYM -1: **chiquillo/a** *n.*

NOTE: This noun comes from the adjective *chico/a* meaning "small."

SYNONYM -2: **chiquitín/a** *n.*

NOTE: This noun comes from the adjective *chico/a* meaning "small."

SYNONYM -3: **crío/a** *m.* • (lit.): a nursing-baby.

SYNONYM -4: **enano/a** *n. (Spain)* short person • (lit.): dwarf.

SYNONYM -5: **gurrumino/a** *n.* • (lit.): weak or sickly person, "whimp."

SYNONYM -6: **mocoso/a** *n.* • (lit.): snotty-nosed person.

SYNONYM -7: **párvulo** *m.* • (lit.): tot.

SYNONYM -8: **pendejo/a** *n. (Argentina).*

SYNONYM -9: **pequeñajo/a** *n.*

NOTE: This noun comes from the adjective *pequeño/a* meaning "small."

SYNONYM -10: **pituso/a** *n.* smurf (from the cartoon characters).

ANTONYM -1: **grandote** *m.*

NOTE: This noun comes from the adjective *grande* meaning "big."

ANTONYM -2: **grandullón/a** *n.* big kid.

NOTE: This noun comes from the adjective *grande* meaning "big."

colarse *v.* **1.** to gate-crash • **2.** *(as seen in lesson two)* to cut in line.

example: Manuel intentó **colarse** en la fiesta de Rosalía.

translation: Manuel tried to **crash** Rosalia's party.

SYNONYM -1: **deslizarse** *v.* • (lit.): to slide, to slip.

SYNONYM -2: **escurrirse** *v.* • (lit.): to drain, to drip, to trickle, to slip.

SYNONYM -3: **meterse delante de** *exp.* • (lit.): to put in front of.

correr *v.* to go fast or faster, to drive fast or faster • (lit.): to run.

example: Quiero **correr** más pero no puedo porque hay mucho tráfico.

translation: I want to **go faster** but I can't because there is a lot of traffic.

SYNONYM -1: **acelerar el paso** *exp.* to speed up • (lit.): to accelerate the step.

SYNONYM -2: **apretar el acelerador** *exp.* to put the pedal to the metal • (lit.): to squeeze the accelerator.

ALSO: **carretera y manta** *exp.* to hit the road • (lit.): road and blanket.

desmadre *m.* chaotic mess.

example: ¡Esta boda es un **desmadre**! Nadie sabe donde sentarse.

translation: This wedding is a **chaotic mess**! Nobody knows where to sit.

ALSO -1: **¡Qué desmadre!** *interj.* What a mess!

ALSO -2: **armar un desmadre** *exp.* to kick up a rumpus.

SYNONYMS: SEE - **gazpacho**, *p. 39*.

dominguero *m.* a bad driver, Sunday driver.

example: Parece que todos los **domingueros** decidieron salir al mismo tiempo.

translation: It looks like all the **Sunday drivers** decided to go out at the same time.

NOTE: This comes from the noun *domingo* meaning "Sunday."

SYNONYM: **bago** *m. (Mexico).*

lata *f.* • **1.** pain in the neck, annoyance, nuisance • **2.** boring person or thing • **3.** long boring speech or conversation • (lit.): tin can.

example: Esta película es una verdadera **lata**.

translation: This movie is so **boring**.

SYNONYM -1: **garrón** *m. (Argentina).*

SYNONYM -2: **moserga** *f.* • (lit.): bore, nuisance.

SYNONYM -3: **rollo** *m.* • (lit.): roll • SEE - *p. 124.*

SYNONYM -4: **tabarra** *f.* • (lit.): bore, nuisance.

ALSO -1: **dar la lata** *exp.* • **1.** to annoy • **2.** to bore • (lit.): to give the can.

ALSO -2: **¡Qué lata!** *interj.* What a pain in the butt! • (lit.): What a tin can!

leñazo *m.* blow, bump, accident • (lit.): large piece of firewood.

example: Ayer Luis se dió un **leñazo** en el coche.

translation: Yesterday Luis had a car **accident**.

SYNONYM -1: **batacazo** *m.* • (lit.): thud.

SYNONYM -2: **golpetazo** *m.* • (lit.): great blow or knock.

VARIATION: **golpazo** *m.*

NOTE: From the verb *golpear* meaning "to hit."

SYNONYM -3: **porrazo** *m.* • (lit.): great blow or knock.

SYNONYM -4: **topetazo** *m.* • (lit.): great blow or knock.

SYNONYM -5: **trancazo** *m.* • (lit.): great blow or knock.

SYNONYM -6: **trompazo** *m.* • (lit.): great blow or knock.

ALSO: **dar/pegar un leñazo** *exp.* to hit something or someone, to have an accident.

¡Olé! *interj. (Spain)* Yippee! Alright!

example: **!Olé!** Vaya gol que ha metido Alvaro.

translation: **Yippee!** What a goal Alvaro just scored!

NOTE: This expression has its roots in the bullfights. It is still the traditional cheer from the audience when a bullfighter makes a good pass.

ALSO: **¡Y olé!** *interj. (Spain).*

SYNONYM: **¡Caramba!** *interj. (Mexico).*

pincharse una llanta *exp.* to get a flat tire • (lit.): to puncture a tire.

example: Ayer llegué tarde a la escuela porque se me **pinchó una llanta**.

translation: Yesterday I arrived late to school because I **got a flat tire**.

NOTE: There are many different terms for "tire" depending on the country:

SYNONYM -1: **caucho** *m. (Venezuela).*

SYNONYM -2: **cubierta** *f. (Argentina / Uruguay).*

SYNONYM -3: **goma** *f. (Argentina / Uruguay).*

SYNONYM -4: **llanta** *f. (Latin America).*

SYNONYM -5: **neumático** *m. (Spain).*

SYNONYM -6: **rueda** *f. (Spain).*

regalito *m.* a lousy present or gift (usually used sarcastically) • (lit.): small gift.

example: ¡Vaya **regalito**! ¡Mi papá me dio un dólar de regalo de cumpleaños!

translation: What a **great gift**! My dad gave me one dollar for my birthday!

rollo *m.* • **1.** ordeal • **2.** long boring speech or conversation • **3.** boring person or thing • **4.** *(Spain)* movie, film, story • (lit.): roll, paper roll.

example (1): ¡Qué **rollo**! ¡Ahora se me descompuso mi carro!

translation: What an **ordeal**! Now my car broke down!

example (2): El discuro de Augusto es tan **rollo** que me estoy quedando dormido.

translation: Augusto's speech is so **boring** I'm falling asleep.

example (3): Ese tipo es un **rollo**. Me estoy quedando dormido de escucharle hablar.

translation: That guy is so **boring**. I'm falling asleep just by listening to him talk.

example (4): Esta noche hay un buen **rollo** en la televisión.

translation: There's a good move on television tonight.

ALSO -1: **meter un rollo** *exp.* to lie, to tell a lie • (lit.): to introduce a roll.

ALSO -2: **¡Qué rollo!** *interj.* How boring!

ALSO -3: **soltar el rollo** *exp.* to talk a lot • (lit.): to set free or let go a roll.

romper a *v.* to burst out, to do something suddenly.

example: Parecía que Agustín iba a **romper a** reir cuando se enteró que ganó la lotería.

translation: It seemed like Agustin was going to **burst out** laughing when he found out he won the lottery.

SYNONYM -1: **echarse a** *v.* • (lit.): to throw oneself to • *echarse a llorar / reir;* to burst out crying / laughing.

SYNONYM -2: **largar** *v. (Argentina)* • (lit.): to release.

SYNONYM -3: **poner a** *v.* • (lit.): to put.

vivo *adj. (Argentina / Uruguay / Spain)* smart, clever, bright • (lit.): alive.

example: Alvaro es un **vivo**. Siempre se sale con la suya.

translation: Alvaro is so **smart**. Everything always goes his way.

SYNONYM -1: **despabilado/a** *adj.*

SYNONYM -2: **despierto/a** *adj.* • (lit.): awaken.

SYNONYM -3: **espabilado/a** *adj. (Spain).*

SYNONYM -4: **listillo/a** *adj.*

NOTE: This comes from the adjective *listo* meaning "clear" or "smart."

SYNONYM -5: **pillo** *adj.* • (lit.): roguish, mischievous.

ANTONYM -1: **adoquín** *adj.* • (lit.): paving block.

ANTONYM -2: **bruto/a** *adj.* • (lit.): stupid, crude.

ANTONYM -3: **cabezota** *adj.* • (lit.): big-headed.

NOTE: This comes from the feminine noun *cabeza* meaning "head."

ANTONYM -4: **tosco/a** *adj.* • (lit.): coarse, crude, unrefined.

ANTONYM -5: **zopenco/a** *adj.* • (lit.): dull, stupid.

Practice the Vocabulary

(*Answers to Lesson 8, p. 183*)

A. Choose the correct synonym of the word(s) in boldface.

1. **azotea**:
   a. head b. ears

2. **chamaco**:
   a. little car b. little boy

3. **colarse**:
   a. to cut in line b. to overpay for something

4. **leñazo**:
   a. piece of wood b. blow, accident

5. **¡Olé!**:
   a. Yippee! b. No way!

6. **desmadre**:
   a. grandmother b. mess

7. **dominguero**:
   a. Sunday driver b. truck driver

8. **vivo**:
   a. stupid person b. smart person

9. **rollo**:
   a. boring b. cake

10. **regalito**:
    a. book b. little surprise

11. **correr**:
    a. to speak   b. to drive fast

12. **¡Qué lata!**:
    a. What a drag!   b. How terrific!

B. Complete the sentences by choosing the appropriate word(s) from the list below. Make all necessary changes.

allá	**desmadre**	**regalito**
azotea	**domingueros**	**rollo**
burro	**lata**	**romper a**
correr	**pinchar**	**vivo**

1. Juan es un ____________________. Nunca hace nada bien.
2. No puedo ____________________ más porque hay mucho tráfico.
3. ¡Este restaurante es un ____________________! No hay organización.
4. Hoy es peligroso salir a la carretera porque hay muchos __________.
5. ¡Qué ____________________! Ese tipo no para de hablar.
6. ¡Qué mala suerte! Se me ____________________ una llanta.
7. ¡Vaya ____________________! Se me descompuso el coche.
8. Esta película es muy aburrida. ¡Es un verdadero ________________!
9. Creo que voy a ____________________ llorar. Nada me sale bien hoy.
10. Federico es un ____________________. Siempre sabe cómo solucionar los problemas.
11. ¡La casa de Andrés está tan ____________________!
12. Parece que ese tipo está mal de la ____________________.

C. Underline the word that best completes the phrase.

1. José es un (**pato**, **jirafa**, **burro**). Nunca hace nada bien.

2. Cuando fuimos a la feria, nos subimos en los (**cacharritos**, **cachupas**, **cántaros**).

3. El parque está lleno de (**chalecos**, **chamacos**, **chatos**).

4. Parece que Alberto está mal de la (**azotea**, **techo**, **suelo**).

5. ¡Qué (**botella**, **lata**, **vaso**)! Empezó a llover.

6. ¡(**Olé**, **Olí**, **Olú**)! Salió el sol.

7. Hoy hay muchos (**luneros**, **domingueros**, **marteros**) en la carretera.

8. ¡Qué (**deshermano**, **desmadre**, **despadre**)! Esto es un verdadero lío.

9. ¡Cuidado! Ese tipo quiere (**colarse**, **colgatarse**, **contarse**) delante tuya.

10. Stefani es muy (**vitalicia**, **viva**, **vista**). Sabe de todo.

11. ¡Qué (**rollo**, **rolla**, **rollizo**)! Esta película es muy aburrida.

12. ¡Me caí de la cama! Creo que voy a (**quebrar**, **romper**, **brincar**) a llorar.

D. Complete the dialogue using the list below.

allá	**correr**	**olé**
azotea	**desmadre**	**regalito**
burro	**domingueros**	**rollo**
cacharritos	**lata**	**romper**
chamacos	**leñazo**	**vivo**
colaban	**llanta**	

Anabel: ¿Cuando vamos a llegar? Yo no tenía ni idea que la feria estaba tan ____________________.

Marcelo: Quisiera poder ____________________ más, pero lo que pasa es que hay muchos ____________________ en la carretera. Ya sabes, la última vez que fui a la feria tardé seis horas porque me dieron un ________________ ...¡se me pinchó una ________________!

Anabel: ¡Qué ____________________!

Marcelo: ¡Creí que iba a ____________________ a llorar! Yo creía que era lo bastante ____________________ como para cambiar la llanta, así que lo hice yo mismo. Pero mientras estaba cambiándola, me dieron un ____________________ en la ____________________ porque un __________________ me tiró una lata de soda desde

su bólido. ¡Qué __________________! ¡Me enojé tanto!

Anabel: ¡Qué __________________! Bueno, yo no creo que tengas que

preocuparte de eso esta vez porque ¡la feria está allí mismo!

Marcelo: __________________ Espero que no haya desmasiados

__________________. El año pasado se __________________

en todos los __________________ más divertidos.

E. DICTATION
Test Your Aural Comprehension

(This dictation can be found in the Appendix on page 192.)

If you are following along with your cassette, you will now hear a series of sentences from the opening dialogue. These sentences will be read by a native speaker at normal conversational speed (which may seem fast to you at first). In addition, the words will be pronounced *as you would actually hear them in a conversation,* oftentimes including some common reductions.

The first time the sentences are presented, simply listen in order to get accustomed to the speed and heavy use of reductions. The sentences will then be read again with a pause after each to give you time to write down what you heard. The third time the sentences are read, follow along with what you have written.

LECCIÓN NUEVE

Esta *tía* está bien *conservada* para su edad.

(trans.): This ***woman*** *looks very* ***youthful*** *for her age.*
(lit.): This ***aunt*** *is very* ***well preserved*** *for her age.*

Lección Nueve

Dialogue in Slang

Esta tía está bien conservada para su edad.

Cecilia: Espero que el **rollo** empiece pronto. **Me revienta** cuando empiezan tarde.

Enrique: Sí, ya sé a lo que te refieres. Dime, ¿Te **enteraste** de qué **se trata** el rollo?

Cecilia: Sí, es muy interesante. **Bueno**, se trata de una **tía** que tiene cincuenta **abriles**, pero que está muy **bien conservada** para su edad y va a un **reventón**. Más tarde esa misma noche, un **barbas** se le acerca y empieza a **charlar** con ella. En solo unos momentos, se enamora de ella porque ella es una **dulzura** de mujer. Unos meses más tarde, **se lía** con el **tío** pero descubre que no es tan **buena onda** como todo el mundo cree. Aparte de ser un **testarudo** y un **huevón**, !descubre que él tiene veinte personalidades y dos de ellas son las de un asesino! Al final, ella no sabe como **deshacerse de** él. ¡Es un verdadero **follón**!

Lesson Nine

Cecilia: I hope the **movie** starts soon. It **bugs me** when they start late.

Enrique: Yeah, I know what you mean. Say, did you ever **find out** what this movie **is about**?

Cecilia: Yes, it's very interesting. **Okay**, it's about a **girl** who is fifty **years old**, but very **well preserved** for her age and goes to a **party**. Later that evening, a **bearded man** starts **chatting** with her. Within moments, he falls in love with her because she's such a **sweetheart**. Months later, she **gets involved** with the **guy** only to discover that he's not such a **good egg** like everyone thought. Aside from being **stubborn** and **a lazy bum**, she discovers that he has twenty personalities and two of them are murderers! So now, she doesn't know how to **get rid of** him. It's a total **mess**!

Vocabulary

abriles (tener ____) *exp.* to be ____ years old • (lit.): to have ____ Aprils.

example: Lola es tan joven. Sólo **tiene 20 abriles**.

translation: Lola is so young. She's only **20 years old**.

ALSO -1: **tener muchas millas** *exp.* to be very old • (lit.): to have many miles.

NOTE: This expression is usually used in reference to an old woman.

ALSO -2: **tener ____ años y muchos meses** *exp.* to be old • (lit.): to be ____ years old and many months more.

SYNONYM: **primaveras (tener ____)** *exp. (Mexico)* • (lit.): to have ____ springtimes.

barbas *m.* bearded man.

example: Augusto siempre ha sido un **barbas**. Parece que no le gusta afeitarse.

translation: Augusto has always been a **bearded man**. It seems like he doesn't like to shave.

SYNONYM -1: **barbado** *m. (Puerto Rico).*

SYNONYM -2: **barbón** *m.*

SYNONYM -3: **barbudo** *m.*

NOTE: These synonyms come from the feminine noun *barba* meaning "beard."

SYNONYM -4: **fulano** *m. (Mexico).*

buena onda *f.* good egg, good person • (lit.): good wave.

example: Agustín es muy **buena onda**. Siempre está dispuesto a ayudar.

translation: Agustín is a **good egg**. He is always willing to help.

SYNONYM -1: **buena gente** *f.* good person • (lit.): good people.

NOTE: The term *buena gente* is commonly used to refer to only one person, although the literal translation is indeed plural. However, when used to refer to a group of people, it is no longer considered slang.

SYNONYM -2: **buenas (estar de)** *adj. (Puerto Rico).*

SYNONYM -3: **buen partido / buena partida** *n. (Cuba).*

SYNONYM -4: **tío enrollado** *m. (Spain)* • (lit.): rolled up uncle (or a person rolled up into one great package).

NOTE: **tío** *m. (Cuba / Spain)* man, "dude."

bueno/a • **1.** *adj.* well... • **2.** *interj.* sure! • **3.** *adj.* bad, nasty • **4.** *adj.* considerable • **5.** *interj.* come off it! • **6.** *adj.* okay • (lit.): good.

example (1): **Bueno**, resulta que Alvaro y Fiona se van de vacaciones a Paris.

translation: **Well**, it so happens that Alvaro and Fiona are going on vacation to Paris.

example (2): ¿Quieres comer en ese restaurante?
¡**Bueno**!

translation: Do you want to eat in that restaurant?
Sure!

example (3): Me siento muy mal. Tengo un **buen** costipado.

translation: I feel sick. I have a **very bad** cold.

example (4): Parece que José tiene una **buena** cantidad de dinero en el banco.

translation: It seems that Jose has a **considerable** amount of money in the bank.

example (5): ¡Me acabo de enterar que mis antepasados eran nobles!
¡**Bueno**! Eso es un poco difícil de creer.

translation: I just found out that my ancestors are royalty!
Come off it! That's a little hard to believe.

example (6): ¿Te gustó la película de anoche?
Bueno. Me gustó más o menos.

translation: Did you like the movie last night?
It was okay. I sort of liked it.

NOTE: In Mexico, using the interjection *bueno* is a common way of answering the telephone.

SYNONYM: **caramba** *interj. (Puerto Rico)* used as a synonym for definition **1**.

charlar *v.* to chat.

example: A Pepa le gusta **charlar** mucho con las amigas.

translation: Pepa loves to **chat** with her friends.

SYNONYM -1: **charlatear** *v.*

SYNONYM -2: **charlotear** *v.*

SYNONYM -3: **cuchichear** *v.*

SYNONYM -4: **parlotear** *v.*

NOTE: This term comes from the verb *parlar* meaning "to talk" or "to chat."

SYNONYM -5: **platicar** *v. (extremely common in Mexico).*

ALSO: **tener una charla** *exp.* to have a conversation.

bien conservado/a (estar) *adj.* to be in good shape for one's age • (lit.): to be well preserved.

example: Julio está muy **bien conservado** para su edad.

translation: Julio is **well preserved** for his age.

VARIATION: **buena conservado/a (estar)** *adj. (Argentina)*

SYNONYM: **buena forma (estar en)** *exp.* • (lit.): to be in good form.

deshacerse de alguien *exp.* to get rid of someone • (lit.): to undo oneself of someone.

example: Juan es tan aburrido. Quería **deshacerme de** él pero no sabía cómo.

translation: Juan is so boring. I wanted to get **rid of** him, but I didn't know how.

SYNONYM: **dar un esquinazo a alguien** *exp.* • (lit.): to give a corner to someone.

ALSO: **deshacerse por uno** *exp.* to go out of one's way for someone, to outdo oneself for someone, to bend over backward for someone • (lit.): to undo oneself for.

dulzura *f.* sweetheart.

example: Lynda es una **dulzura**. Siempre está sonriendo.

translation: Lynda is a **sweetheart**. She is always smiling.

SYNONYM -1: **amor** *m.* • (lit.): love.

SYNONYM -2: **bombón** *m.* • (lit.): a type of chocolate candy.

SYNONYM -3: **caramelo** *m.* • (lit.): candy.

SYNONYM -4: **ternura** *f.* • (lit.): tenderness.

enterarse *v.* to find out • (lit.): to inform oneself.

example: ¿**Te enteraste** de cómo se llega a la casa de Alfredo?

translation: Did you **find out** how get to Alfredo's house?

follón *m.* • **1.** mess, jam • **2.** trouble, uproar.

example (1): El tráfico de Chicago es un **follón**.

translation: The traffic in Chicago is a **mess**.

example (2): Si nuestro equipo pierde el partido se va a armar un gran **follón**.

translation: If our team loses the games, there is going to be an **uproar** here.

SYNONYMS: SEE - **gazpacho**, *p. 39*.

ALSO -1: **armar un follón** *exp.* to kick up a rumpus.

ALSO -2: ¡**Menudo follón!** *exp.* What a mess!

ALSO -3: ¡**Qué follón**! *exp.* What a mess!

huevón *adj.* lazy.

example: Mario es un **huevón**. Nunca hace nada.

translation: Mario is a **lazy bum**. He never does anything.

SYNONYM -1: **dejado/a** *adj.* • (lit.): left (from the verb *dejar* meaning "to leave [something]").

SYNONYM -2: **flojo/a** *adj. & n.* • (lit.): lazy, idle.

SYNONYM -3: **parado/a** *adj. (Spain).*

NOTE: This is pronounced: *parao / parah* in Spain.

SYNONYM -4: **vago/a** *adj. (Spain)* • (lit.): vague.

ALSO: **hacer la hueva** *exp.* not to lift a finger, to do nothing • (lit.): to make a female egg.

liarse *v.* to get involved (with someone), to go out with • (lit.): to tie up, to wrap up.

example: Parece que Alfonso se ha **liado** con Lynda.

translation: It seems like Alfonso is **involved** with Lynda.

SYNONYM -1: **engancharse** *v. (Argentina)* • (lit.): to get hooked up (with someone).

SYNONYM -2: **enrollarse** *v.* • (lit.): to roll up.

SYNONYM -3: **juntarse** *v.* • (lit.): to join, to unite.

SYNONYM -4: **ligarse** *v. (Cuba / Mexico)* • (lit.): to tie oneself up (with someone).

ALSO: **liarse a golpes** *exp.* to come to blows.

reventón *m.* party • (lit.): bursting, explosion.

example: Esta noche vamos a ir a un **reventón**.

translation: Tonight we are going to a **party**.

SYNONYMS: SEE - **pachanga**, *p. 23*.

reventar *v.* • **1.** to annoy, to bug • **2.** to tire someone out • (lit.): to burst.

example (1): Me **revienta** cuando llegas tarde.

translation: It **bugs** me when you're late.

example (2): ¡Ernesto come tanto que un día de estos ¡va a **reventar**!

translation: Pedro eats so much that one of these days he's going to **explode**!

SYNONYM: **matar** *v. (Spain)* • (lit.): to kill.

rollo *m. (Spain)* movie, story • (lit.): roll.

example: !Este **rollo** es demasiado largo!

translation: This **movie** is too long!

NOTE -1: As you've probably noticed, the term *rollo* was used in the previous lesson and is used again here due to its numerous meanings and extreme popularity among Spanish speakers.

NOTE -2: For other meanings of *rollo*, see *p. 124*

ALSO -1: ¡**Qué rollo**! *interj.* How boring!

ALSO -2: **meter un rollo** *exp.* to tell a lie • (lit.): to introduce (put in) a roll.

ALSO (3): **soltar el rollo** *exp.* to talk a lot, to babble on • (lit.): to let go a roll.

testarudo *adj.* stubborn, headstrong.

example: Javier es un **testarudo**. Cuando se le mete una idea en la cabeza, nunca cambia de opinión.

translation: Javier is so **stubborn**. When he gets an idea in his head, he never changes his mind.

NOTE: This comes from the feminine latin word *testa* meaning "head."

SYNONYM -1: **cabezón** *adj.* • **1.** headstrong • **2.** big-headed.

NOTE: This term comes from the feminine noun *cabeza* meaning "head."

SYNONYM -2: **machacón** *adj.* • (lit.): boring, tiresome.

SYNONYM -3: **terco** *adj.* • (lit.): obstinate, stubborn.

SYNONYM -4: **tozudo** *adj.* • (lit.): obstinate, stubborn.

tía *f. (Spain / Cuba)* girl, "chick" • (lit.): type.

example: ¡Mira esa **tipa**! ¡Me gusta su minifalda!

translation: Look at that **chick**! I like her miniskirt!

SYNONYM -1: **mina** *f. (Argentina)*

SYNONYM -2: **tipa** *f.* • (lit.): aunt.

ANTONYM -1: **tío** *m. (Cuba / Spain)* guy, "dude" • (lit.): uncle.

ANTONYM -2: **tipo** *m.* • (lit.): type.

tratar(se) + de *exp.* to be about, to pertain to • (lit.): to treat oneself of.

example (1): Esta obra de teatro **trata de** Don Quijote.

translation: This play **is about** Don Quixote.

example (2): ¿De qué **se trata**?

translation: What **is this about**?

Practice the Vocabulary

(Answers to Lesson 9, p. 184)

A. Underline the correct synonym of the word(s) in boldface.

1. **charlar**:
   a. to chat b. to sign

2. **testarudo**:
   a. tasty b. stubborn

3. **barbas**:
   a. barbaric b. bearded man

4. **bien conservado (estar)**:
   a. to be well preserved b. to be very conservative

5. **huevón**:
   a. lazy bum b. large omelette

6. **reventón**:
   a. explosion b. party

7. **dulzura**:
   a. sweetheart b. candy

8. **enterarse**:
   a. to find out b. to avoid

9. **rollo**:
   a. roll of bread b. movie

10. **reventar**:
    a. to annoy b. to like

11. **abriles ______ (tener)**:
    a. to be ______ years old b. to be ______ months old

12. **buena onda**:
    a. good egg b. good morning

B. Complete the phrases by choosing the appropriate words from the list below. Make all necessary changes.

barbas	**dulzura**	**rollo**
bueno	**follón**	**testarudo**
charlar	**huevón**	**tía**
conservado	**liarse**	**tratar(se)**

1. Me encanta ____________________ con Ana porque siempre tiene algo interesante que contar.

2. Luis en un ____________________ . Nunca tiene ganas de trabajar.

3. Lynda es una ____________________ de mujer. Siempre está contenta.

4. ____________________ , resulta que Antonio consiguió un trabajo en Londres.

5. Manuel está muy bien ____________________ para su edad.

6. Javier no se afeita nunca. Es un ____________________ .

7. Rafael es un ____________________ . Nunca cambia de opinión.

8. Parece que Alfredo se ha ____________________ con Susan.

9. ¡Mira esa ____________________ ! ¡Me encanta su vestido!

10. No me gusta este ____________________ . Prefiero una película de miedo.

11. El tráfico de Chicago es un verdadero ____________________ .

12. Esta película ____________________ de Don Quijote.

C. Match the Spanish with the English translation by writing the corresponding letter of the answer in the box.

☐ 1. Don Quixote was a bearded man.

☐ 2. If our team loses the games, there is going to be an uproar here.

☐ 3. Lynda loves to chat with Patricia.

☐ 4. Eduardo is a good egg.

☐ 5. Sara is such a sweetheart.

☐ 6. Felipe is a lazy bum.

☐ 7. Tonight we're going to a party.

☐ 8. Look at that beautiful girl!

☐ 9. This movie is so long.

☐ 10. It bugs me when you're late.

☐ 11. Carlos is very stubborn.

☐ 12. It looks like Alvaro is involved with Fiona.

A. **Eduardo es buena onda.**

B. **Parece que Alvaro está liado con Fiona.**

C. **Carlos es muy testarudo.**

D. **Felipe es un huevón.**

E. **Me revienta cuando llegas tarde.**

F. **¡Mira qué tía más bonita!**

G. **Este rollo es muy largo.**

H. **Esta noche vamos a un reventón.**

I. **Sara es una dulzura.**

J. **Don Quijote era un barbas.**

K. **A Lynda le encanta charlar con Patricia.**

L. **Si nuestro equipo pierde el partido se va a armar un gran follón.**

D. WORD SEARCH

Circle the words in the cube on page 144 that fit the following expressions. Words may be spelled up, down, or across.

barbas	**enterarse**	**reventón**
bueno	**follón**	**rollo**
charlar	**huevón**	**testarudo**
conservado	**liarse**	**tía**
deshacerse	**onda**	**tratarse**
dulzura	**reventar**	

1. ______ *m.* bearded man.

2. **buena** ______ *f.* good egg, good person • (lit.): good wave.

3. ______ • **1.** *adj.* well… • **2.** *interj.* fine! • **3.** *adj.* bad, nasty • **4.** *adj.* considerable • **5.** *interj.* come off it! • **6.** *adj.* okay • (lit.): good.

4. ______ *v.* to chat.

5. **bien** ______ **(estar)** *adj.* to be in good shape for one's age • (lit.): to be well preserved.

6. ______ **de alguien** *exp.* to get rid of someone • (lit.): to undo oneself of someone.

7. ______ *f.* sweetheart.

8. ______ *v.* to find out • (lit.): to inform oneself.

9. ______ *m.* • **1.** mess, jam • **2.** trouble, uprorar.

10. ______ *m.* lazy

11. ______ *v.* to get involved with [someone], to go out with • (lit.): to tie up, to wrap up.

12. ______ *m.* party • (lit.): bursting, explosion.

13. ______ *v.* • **1.** to annoy, to bug • **2.** to tire someone out • (lit.): to burst.

14. ______ *m.* • **1.** movie, story • **2.** long boring speech or conversation • **3.** ordeal • **4.** boring person or thing • (lit.): roll.

15. ______ *adj.* stubborn, headstrong.

16. ______ *f.* girl, "chick" • (lit.): aunt.

17. ______ **de** *exp.* to be about, to pertain to.

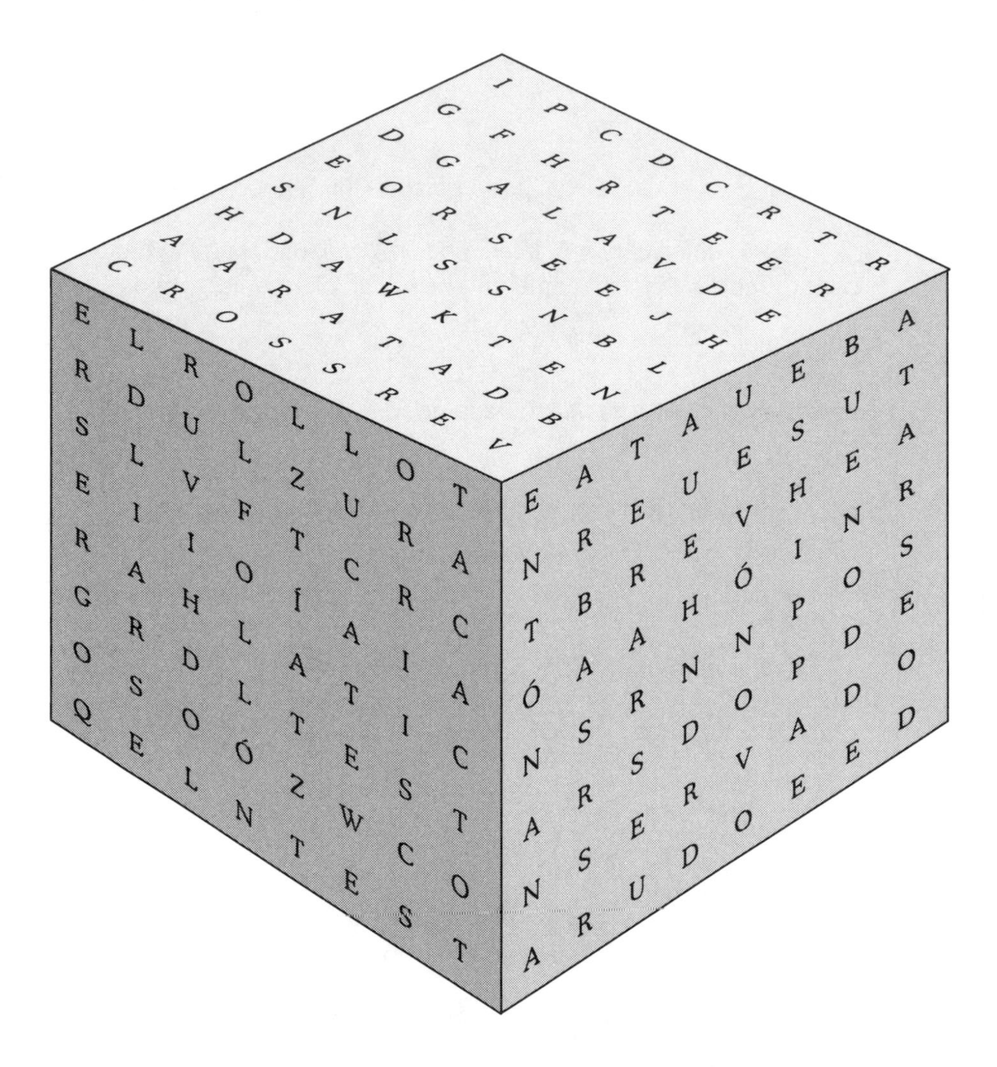

E. DICTATION
Test Your Aural Comprehension

(This dictation can be found in the Appendix on page 193.)

If you are following along with your cassette, you will now hear a series of sentences from the opening dialogue. These sentences will be read by a native speaker at normal conversational speed (which may seem fast to you at first). In addition, the words will be pronounced *as you would actually hear them in a conversation,* oftentimes including some common reductions.

The first time the sentences are presented, simply listen in order to get accustomed to the speed and heavy use of reductions. The sentences will then be read again with a pause after each to give you time to write down what you heard. The third time the sentences are read, follow along with what you have written.

LECCIÓN DIEZ

¡Ese *tío* tiene mucha *pasta*!

(trans.): This ***guy*** *has a lot of* ***money****!*
(lit.): This ***uncle*** *has a lot of* ***pasta****!*

Lección Diez

Dialogue in Slang

¡Ese tío tiene mucha pasta!

Sandra: ¿Qué te pasa? ¡Pareces que estás **brava** hoy! ¿No te lo pasaste bien anoche en tu **cita sorpresa**?

Luisa: Bueno, al principio parecía que iba a ser un **pedazo** de cita. Marco vino a mi **nido** a eso de las ocho de la noche. Yo **tenía pavor** de que iba a ser un **bobo** o un **gordinflón**, o un **canijo**, pero sin embargo, vi a un verdadero **galán** salir del coche y caminar hacia mi casa. ¡Yo estaba **supercontenta**! Como es un **matasanos**, yo sabía que tenía que ser un **listillo**, y al ver su auto y sus **trapos**, se veía que era un gran **gozador**.

Sandra: Entonces, ¿Cual es el problema?

Luisa: Le pregunté que si quería algo de **tragar** y dijo que no. Entonces le pregunté que si quería ir al cine o a **callejear** o a tomar un helado. Pero en vez de decir vale, a cualquiera de mis sugerencias, parece que no tenía ganas de hacer nada.

Sandra: ¡Qué tipo más **aguafiestas**!

Luisa: Así que nos quedamos en mi **castillo** y charlamos un rato, pero estuve muy aburrida porque ese **tío** es un verdadero **robot**. Parece que no tiene personalidad. Y como tiene tanta **pasta**, es un **creído**. ¡Tenía muchas ganas de decirle **chao**!

Lesson Ten

Sandra: What's wrong? You seem **upset** today! Didn't you have a good time last night on your **blind date**?

Luisa: Well, at first it seemed like it was going to be a **great** date. Marco came to my **house** around 8:00pm. I **was scared** he was either going to be an **idiot** or a **fat pig**, or a **really skinny guy** but instead, I saw a real **hunk** get out of his car and walk toward my house. I was **ultra happy**! Since he's a **doctor**, I knew he must be very **smart**, and judging by his **clothes**, he's definitely a **big spender**.

Sandra: Then, what's the problem?

Luisa I asked him if he wanted to get something **to eat** and he said no. So, I asked him if he'd like to go to a movie, or **to take a walk**, or to get some ice cream. But instead of saying okay to any of my suggestions, he just didn't feel like doing anything.

Sandra: What a **stick in the mud**!

Luisa: So we just stayed at my **house** and chatted for a while, but I was really bored because this **guy** is a total **deadhead**. He didn't show any personality. And because he has so much **money**, he's a **snob**. I couldn't wait to say **see ya**!

Vocabulary

aguafiestas *m.* party-pooper, stick in the mud, kill-joy • (lit.): water-festival (referring to someone who "throws water on a festival" as one would throw on a fire to extinguish it).

example: A mi novio no le gusta ir a bailar. ¡Es un verdadero **aguafiestas**!

translation: My boyfriend never likes to go out dancing. He's such a **stick in the mud**!

SYNONYM -1: **aguado/a** *n. (Mexico).*

SYNONYM -2: **chocante** *m. (Mexico).*

SYNONYM -3: **embolante** *m. (Argentina).*

bobo/a *n.* idiot, fool.

example: Carlos es un **bobo**. No sabe ni atarse los cordones de los zapatos.

translation: Carlos is an **idiot**. He doesn't even know how to tie his shoes.

VARIATION: **bobo de capirote** *exp.* a complete idiot • (lit.): stupid in the hat.

SYNONYM -1: **asno** *adj.* • (lit.): donkey.

SYNONYM -2: **atontado/a** *adj.* • (lit.): stupid person.

SYNONYM -3: **bobazo** *m. (Argentina).*

SYNONYM -4: **burro** *adj.* • (lit.): donkey – SEE: *burro, p. 120.*

SYNONYM -5: **ganso** *adj.* • (lit.): goose.

SYNONYM -6: **mentecato/a** *adj.* • (lit.): silly, foolish.

SYNONYM -7: **pasmarote** *adj.* • (lit.): silly, foolish.

SYNONYM -8: **patoso/a** *adj.* • (lit.): boring, dull.

SYNONYM -9: **tonto/a** *adj.* • (lit.): stupid person.

SYNONYM -10: **zopenco/a** *adj.* • (lit.): dull, stupid.

SYNONYM -11: **zoquete** *adj.* • (lit.): chump, block (of wood).

ANTONYM -1: **listillo/a** *adj. (Spain)* • (lit.): small clever person.

ANTONYM -2: **pillo** *adj.* • (lit.): roguish, mischievous, rascally.

ANTONYM -3: **vivo/a** *adj.* clever, smart • (lit.): alive.

bravo/a *adj.* upset, angry • (lit.): fierce, ferocious.

example: Lucía está **brava** hoy porque no durmió bien anoche.

translation: Lucia is **upset** today because she didn't sleep well last night.

ALSO: ¡**Bravo**! *interj.* Well done!

SYNONYM -1: **cabreado/a** *adj. (Spain).*

SYNONYM -2: **embolado/a** *adj. (Argentina).*

callejear *v.* to take a walk.

example: Cuando hace sol me gusta **callejear**.

translation: When it's sunny outside, I enjoy going for a **walk**.

SYNONYM: **dar una vuelta** *exp.*to go for a walk • (lit.): to give around.

canijo/a *adj.* • **1.** very skinny person • **2.** feeble, frail, sickly.

example: Ese tipo es un verdadero **canijo**. Parece que nunca come.

translation: That guy is **really skinny**. It looks like he never eats.

SYNONYM -1: **esqueleto** *m. (Puerto Rico / Cuba)*• (lit.): skeleton.

SYNONYM -2: **flacuyo** *adj. (Argentina).*

castillo *m.* home, house • (lit.): castle.

example: ¿Te gusta mi **castillo** nuevo? Tiene cuatro dormitorios.

translation: Do you like my new **house**? It has four bedrooms.

SYNONYM -1: **hogar** *m.* • (lit.): home.

SYNONYM -2: **morada** *f.* • (lit.): home.

SYNONYM -3: **nido** *m.* • (lit.): nest.

chao *interj.* good-bye.

example: ¡**Chao**! ¡Hasta la vista!

translation: **Good-bye**! See ya!

NOTE: This slang term comes from the Italian word "ciao" meaning "good-bye" and is extremely popular among Spanish speakers as well as French.

NOTE: In Argentina, this is spelled *chau.*

cita sorpresa *exp.* blind date • (lit.): surprised date.

example: Estoy nervioso porque mañana tengo una **cita sorpresa**.

translation: I'm nervous because I have a **blind date** tomorrow.

SYNONYM -1: **cita a ciegas** *f. (Spain)* • (lit.): blind date.

SYNONYM -2: **cita amorosa** *f. (Mexico)* • (lit.): love date.

creído/a *adj.* snob, conceited person • (lit.): thought or believed.

example: Manuel es un **creído**. Se cree que es mejor que nadie.

translation: Manuel is a **snob**. He thinks he's better than anybody else.

SYNONYM -1: **esnob** *m.*

SYNONYM -2: **snob** *m.*

SYNONYM -3: **zarpado/a** *n. (Argentina).*

galán *adj.* hunk, good-looking guy.

example: Claudio es un **galán**. Se nota que se cuida.

translation: Claudio is a **hunk**. You can tell he takes care of himself.

SYNONYM -1: **chorbo** *adj. (Spain).*

SYNONYM -2: **gallardo** *adj.* • (lit.): elegant, graceful.

NOTE: There is no feminine form of this adjective since it can only refer to a man.

SYNONYM -3: **majo** *adj.* • (lit.): showy, flashy, dressed up.

SYNONYM -4: **tío bueno** *m. (Spain).*

gordinflón *adj.* fat pig, obese person.

example: Darío es un **gordinflón**. Parece que nunca para de comer.

translation: Darío is a **fat pig**. It seems like he never stops eating.

SYNONYM -1: **mofletudo/a** *adj.* • (lit.): chubby-cheeked.

SYNONYM -2: **rechoncho/a** *adj.* • (lit.): chubby, tubby.

SYNONYM -3: **regordete** *adj.*

NOTE: This comes from the adjective *gordo/a* meaning "fat."

SYNONYM -4: **tripón** *adj.*

NOTE: This comes from the feminine noun *tripa* meaning "tripe," "guts" or "stomach."

ANTONYM: **canijo** *adj.* skinny person.

gozador/a *adj.* big spender, person who likes to have fun all the time.

example: Francisco es un gran **gozador**. Le encanta pasarlo bien.

translation: Francisco is such a **big spender**. He loves to have fun.

NOTE: This comes from the verb *gozar* meaning "to enjoy."

SYNONYM -1: **gastador** *m. (Argentina / Cuba).*

SYNONYM -2: **maniroto** *m. (Spain).*

listillo/a *adj. (Spain)* smart, clever person.

example: David es un **listillo**. Siempre tiene la respuesta adecuada.

translation: David is so **smart**. He always has the right answer.

SYNONYM -1: **agosado/a** *adj. (Puerto Rico / Cuban).*

NOTE: In Puerto Rico and Cuba, this is pronounced: *agosao / agosah.*

SYNONYM -2: **avispado/a** *adj.* • (lit.): clever, sharp.

NOTE: This comes from the term *avispa* meaning "wasp."

SYNONYM -3: **despabilado/a** *adj.* • (lit.): awakened.

NOTE: This comes from the verb *despavilar* meaning "to wake up."

SYNONYM -4: **pillo** *adj.* • (lit.): roguish, mischievous.

SYNONYM -5: **vivo/a** *adj.* • (lit.): alive.

ANTONYM -1: **adoquín** *m.* jerk, fool, moron, simpleton • (lit.): paving block.

ANTONYM -2: **bruto/a** *adj.* • (lit.): stupid, crude.

ANTONYM -3: **cabezota** *adj.*

NOTE: This comes from the feminine noun *cabeza* meaning "head." The suffix *-ota* is commonly used to modify the meaning of the noun changing it literally to "big head."

ANTONYM -4: **tosco/a** *adj.* • (lit.): coarse, crude, unrefined.

ANTONYM -5: **zopenco/a** *adj.* • (lit.): dull, stupid.

matasanos *m.* doctor • (lit.): killer of healthy people (from the verb *matar* meaning "to kill" and *sano* meaning "heath").

example: El marido de Gloria es un **matasanos**.

translation: Gloria's husband is a **doctor**.

NOTE: Although this term literally has a negative meaning, it is commonly used in jest to refer to a doctor in general.

SYNONYM: **doc** *m. (Argentina)*.

nido *m.* home, house, place • (lit.): nest.

example: !Oye María! ¿Por qué no vamos a mi **nido** a ver la televisión?

translation: Hey, Maria! Why don't we go to my **place** to watch TV?

ALSO: **haberse caído de un nido** *exp.* to be very gullible • (lit.): to have just fallen from the nest.

SYNONYM -1: **bulin** *m. (Argentina)*.

SYNONYM -2: **castillo** *m.* • (lit.): castle.

SYNONYM -3: **cobijo** *m.* • (lit.): shelter.

SYNONYM -4: **morada** *f.* • (lit.): home.

SYNONYM -5: **palacio** *m.* • (lit.): palace.

SYNONYM -6: **techo** *m.* • (lit.): roof.

pavor (tener) *exp.* to be scared.

example: Sara **tenía pavor** de ir a la escuela el primer día.

translation: Sara was **scared** to go to school on the first day.

SYNONYM: **temblando (estar)** *adj.* • (lit.): to be trembling.

ALSO: **temblar de miedo** *exp.* • (lit.): to shake with fear.

pedazo de *adj.* great (when used before a noun) • (lit.): piece.

example: Alberto se acaba de comprar un **pedazo** de coche.

translation: Alberto just bought a **great** car.

ALSO: **pedazo de pan (ser un)** *exp.* to be very kind or easy-going • (lit.): to be a piece of bread.

SYNONYM: **pasada de** *adj. (Spain)* • (lit.): a passage of.

pasta *f.* money, "dough" • (lit.): pasta.

example: Se nota que Javier tiene **pasta**. Mira su coche.

translation: You can tell Javier is loaded with **money**. Look at his house.

SYNONYMS: SEE - **lana**, *p. 39*.

robot *m.* deadhead, person who doesn't show his / her feelings, apathetic person • (lit.): robot.

example: Julio es un **robot**. Nunca se rie.

translation: Julio is a **deadhead**. He never laughs.

supercontento/a (estar) *adj.* ultra happy.

example: Ernesto está **supercontento** con su motocicleta nueva.

translation: Ernesto is **ultra happy** with his new motorcycle.

ALSO: **pegando saltos (estar)** *exp.* to be jumping for joy • (lit.): to be jumping.

tipo *m.* guy, "dude" • (lit.): type.

example: ¡Ese **tipo** está loco!

translation: That **guy** is crazy!

SYNONYM: **tío** *m. (Spain)* • (lit.): uncle.

ANTONYM: **tipa** *f.* girl, "chick."

tragar *v.* • **1.** to eat • **2.** to drink • (lit.): to swallow.

example: ¿Tienes hambre? ¿Quieres algo de **tragar**?

translation: Are you hungry? Do you want something to **eat**?

SYNONYM -1: **embuchar** *v.* to eat • (lit.): to cram food into the beak of a bird.

SYNONYM -2: **jalar** *v. (Spain).*

SYNONYM -3: **jamar** *v.*

SYNONYM -4: **morfar** *v. (Argentina).*

SYNONYM -5: **papear** *v. (Spain).*

SYNONYM -6: **zampar** *v.* • (lit.): to stuff or cram (food) down, to gobble down.

trapos *m.* clothes • (lit.): rags.

example: Manuela tiene unos **trapos** muy bonitos.

translation: Manuela has very nice **clothes**.

SYNONYM -1: **paños** *m.* • (lit.): rags.

SYNONYM -2: **pilchas** *f.pl. (Argentina).*

SYNONYM -3: **ropaje** *m.* • (lit.): robes.

ALSO -1: **poner a uno como un trapo** *exp.* to give someone a severe reprimand • (lit.): to put oneself like an old rug.

ALSO -2: **sacar los trapos a relucir** *exp.* to air one's dirty laundry in public • (lit.): to take one's dirty laundry to shine.

Practice the Vocabulary 

(Answers to Lesson 10, p. 186)

A. Fill in the blank with the appropriate word that best completes the phrase.

aguafiestas	**galán**	**pasta**
bravo	**gozador**	**robot**
canijo	**matasanos**	**supercontento**
cita sorpresa	**pavor**	**tragar**

1. Sergio es un ________________ . Cuando él llegó se acabó la fiesta.
2. Antonio es un gran ________________ . Le encanta gastar dinero.
3. Creo que Juan es un ________________ porque trabaja en un hospital.
4. Julio es un ________________ . Nunca se rie.
5. Mañana tengo una ________________ . Estoy muy nervioso.
6. ¿No te lo pasaste bien anoche en tu ________________?
7. Tengo ________________ de volar en avión.
8. Parece que Jorge tiene mucha ________________ porque siempre usa ropa cara.
9. Estoy ________________ porque me ha tocado la lotería.
10. Mi padre estaba ________________ porque tomé prestado su auto sin su permiso.
11. Ese tipo es un ________________ . Parece un palillo de dientes.
12. Manolo está muy gordo porque le encanta ________________ .

B. Underline the correct definition of the word in boldface.

1. **bobo**:
   a. dumb — b. smart

2. **callejear**:
   a. to build a house — b. to take a walk

3. **castillo**:
   a. home — b. small cat

4. **chao**:
   a. hello — b. good-bye

5. **creído**:
   a. snob — b. shy person

6. **gordinflón**:
   a. thin person — b. obese person

7. **listillo**:
   a. clever person — b. stupid person

8. **nido**:
   a. home — b. noise

9. **pedazo (de)**:
   a. great — b. lousy

10. **robot**:
    a. outgoing person — b. deadhead

11. **tío**:
    a. man — b. little boy

12. **trapos**:
    a. shoes — b. clothes

C. Underline the appropriate word that best completes the phrase.

1. Alejandro es tan (**bobo**, **bubo**) que no sabe ni usar la cuchara.

2. Cuando hace buen día me encanta (**calibrar**, **callejear**).

3. Siempre llego a mi (**castillo**, **castela**) a las cinco de la tarde.

4. Estoy (**supercontento**, **superatento**) porque gané la lotería.

5. Esta noche tengo una (**cita sorpresa**, **cita ciega**).

6. Mario es un (**creyente**, **creído**). Cree ser mejor que nadie.

7. Alfredo es un verdadero (**galano**, **galán**).

8. A Paco le encanta viajar. Es un verdadero (**gozador**, **gollete**).

9. Agustín es un (**matasanos**, **matamoscas**). Trabaja en un hospital.

10. ¡Mira qué (**pedazo**, **trozo**) de coche se ha comprado Marcelo!

11. Rafael tiene mucha (**planta**, **plata**).

12. A David le gusta (**tragar**, **atrapar**). Por eso está tan gordo.

D. CROSSWORD

Fill in the crossword puzzle on page 163 by choosing the correct word(s) from the list below.

aguafiestas	**galán**	**pedazo**
bobo	**gozador**	**robot**
brava	**listillo**	**tipo**
callejear	**matasanos**	**tragar**
castillo	**nido**	**trapos**
chao	**pasta**	
cita	**pavor**	

ACROSS

3. example: Cuando hace sol me gusta ______.
   translation: When it's sunny outside, I enjoy going for a **walk**.

14. example: Alberto se acaba de comprar un ______ de coche.
    translation: Alberto just bought a **great** car.

18. example: Lucía está ______ hoy porque no durmió bien anoche.
    translation: Lucia is **upset** today because she didn't sleep well last night.

28. example: El marido de Gloria es un ______.
    translation: Gloria's husband is a **doctor**.

34. example: Se nota que Javier tiene ______. Mira su coche.
    translation: You can tell Javier is loaded with **money**. Look at his house.

35. example: ¿Tienes hambre? ¿Quieres algo de ______?

translation: Are you hungry? Do you want something to **eat**?

39. example: Claudio es un ______. Se nota que se cuida.

translation: Claudio is such a **hunk**. You can tell he takes care of himself.

45. example: Carlos es un ______. No sabe ni atarse los cordones de los zapatos.

translation: Carlos is an **idiot**. He doesn't even know how to tie his shoes.

49. example: David es un _________. Siempre tiene la respuesta adecuada.

translation: David is so **smart**. He always has the right answer.

54. example: ¡Ese ______ está loco!

translation: That **guy** is crazy!

55. example: Julio es un ______. Nunca se rie.

translation: Julio is a **deadhead**. He never laughs.

DOWN

3. example: ¡______! ¡Hasta la vista!

translation: **Good-bye**! See ya!

9. example: Los padres de Luis son unos ______. Nos dijeron que saliéramos de la casa.

translation: Luis's parents are **sticks in the mud**. They told us to get out of their house.

21. example: Estoy nervioso porque mañana tengo una ______.

translation: I'm nervous because I have a **blind date** tomorrow.

26. example: ¿Te gusta mi ______ nuevo? Tiene cuatro dormitorios.

translation: Do you like my new **house**? It has four bedrooms.

35. example: Manuela tiene unos ______ muy bonitos.

translation: Manuela has very nice **clothes**.

40. example: Sara tiene ______ de ir a la escuela el primer día.

translation: Sara was **scared** to go to school on the first day.

42. example: Francisco es un gran ______. Le encanta pasarlo bien.

translation: Francisco is such a **big spender**. He loves to have a good time.

47. example: Vamos a comer a mi ______.

translation: Let's go eat at my **house**.

CROSSWORD PUZZLE

3 9 14 18 21 26 28 34 35 39 40 42 45 47 49 54 55

E. DICTATION
Test Your Aural Comprehension

(This dictation can be found in the Appendix on page 193.)

If you are following along with your cassette, you will now hear a series of sentences from the opening dialogue. These sentences will be read by a native speaker at normal conversational speed (which may seem fast to you at first). In addition, the words will be pronounced *as you would actually hear them in a conversation,* oftentimes including some common reductions.

The first time the sentences are presented, simply listen in order to get accustomed to the speed and heavy use of reductions. The sentences will then be read again with a pause after each to give you time to write down what you heard. The third time the sentences are read, follow along with what you have written.

REVIEW EXAM FOR LESSONS 6-10

(Answers to Review, p. 188)

A. Underline the definition of the word(s) in boldface.

1. **antenas**:
   a. hands — b. ears
2. **coco**:
   a. head — b. hair
3. **ardilla**:
   a. smart person — b. stupid person
4. **vacilar**:
   a. to joke around — b. to be serious about something
5. **azotea**:
   a. head — b. ears
6. **chamaco**:
   a. little car — b. little boy
7. **testarudo**:
   a. tasty — b. stubborn
8. **buena onda**:
   a. good egg — b. good morning
9. **huevón**:
   a. lazy bum — b. large omelette
10. **matasanos**:
    a. doctor — b. nurse
11. **canijo**:
    a. skinny person — b. obese person

12. **caradura**:
   a. arrogant person   b. shy person

13. **cochazo**:
   a. old jalopy   b. great car

14. **¡Vaya!**:
   a. How about that!   b. Let's go!

15. **cacharro**:
   a. great car   b. old jalopy

16. **menearse**:
   a. to dance   b. to jump

17. **narizón**:
   a. person with a big nose   b. person with a flat nose

18. **malísimamente**:
   a. fantastically   b. really badly

19. **rollo**:
   a. something boring   b. a kind of bread

20. **¡Qué lata!**:
   a. What a drag!   b. How terrific!

21. **barbas**:
   a. barbaric   b. bearded man

22. **charlar**:
   a. to sing   b. to chat

23. **supercontento**:
   a. depressed   b. ultra happy

B. Complete the following phrases by choosing the appropriate word from the list below. Make all necessary changes.

aguafiestas	**gozador**	**narizón**
carroza	**leñazo**	**renacuajos**
domingueros	**lija**	**reventón**
gordinflón	**manitas**	**rollo**

1. Javier se ha convertido en un ________________ de tanto comer.
2. No me gusta ir a fiestas con Paco porque es un ________________ .
3. Ten cuidado en la carretera porque hay muchos ______________ .
4. ¡Mira que ________________ tiene ese tipo.
5. Juan es un ________________ . Lo sabe arreglar todo.
6. Esta película es muy aburrida. Es un verdadero ______________ .
7. El padre de José Luis en una ________________ . Tiene 85 años.
8. Lo pasé muy bien en el ________________ de anoche.
9. Sergio tiene dos ________________ . Uno de dos años y el otro de tres.
10. A Manuel le gusta darse ________________ .
11. Ayer me di un ________________ con mi coche.
12. La gente dice que soy un ________________ porque me gusta pasarlo bien.

C. Match the Spanish with the English translation by writing the corresponding letter of the answer in the box.

☐ 1. Look what a great car Gerardo has!

☐ 2. My English teacher wears glasses.

☐ 3. Daniel always hogs the ball.

☐ 4. Thomas is my best buddy.

☐ 5. That kid is trying to sneak into the theater.

☐ 6. Yippee! I just won the game!

☐ 7. Marco looks young for his age.

☐ 8. I love to chat with my mother.

☐ 9. What a mess!

☐ 10. Sonia is very upset today.

☐ 11. Claudio is a real snob.

☐ 12. That guy's crazy!

A. **¡Ese tío está loco!**

B. **Sonia está muy brava hoy.**

C. **Marco está muy bien convervado para su edad.**

D. **¡Qué follón!**

E. **Me encanta charlar con mi madre.**

F. **Claudio es un verdadero creído.**

G. **¡Mira que pedazo de coche tiene Gerardo!**

H. **Tomás es mi mejor amiguete.**

I. **Mi profesor de inglés es un cuatroojos.**

J. **¡Olé! ¡Acabo de ganar la lotería!**

K. **Daniel siempre es un chupón.**

L. **Ese niño esta intentando colarse en el teatro.**

D. Underline the appropriate word that best completes the phrase.

1. ¿Quieres venir a mi (**nino**, **nido**, **nado**) a cenar esta noche?

2. Estoy muy ocupado. Tengo una (**pila**, **bateria**, **polo**) de cosas que hacer.

3. Marcelo es un gran (**bailante**, **bailón**, **bailadero**).

4. Maradona (**metió**, **mandó**, **mentó**) dos goles en el partido en ayer.

5. ¡Esto es un (**despadre**, **deshijo**, **desmadre**)! No hay organización.

6. ¡Qué (**lata**, **latura**, **lato**)! Esta película es demasiado larga.

7. Papá Noel es un (**barbero**, **barbas**, **barbonero**).

8. Esa (**tía**, **sobrina**, **gallina**) está muy buena. ¡Mira qué piernas!

9. Parece que Juan nunca come. Es un (**cántaro**, **canijo**, **canoso**).

10. Gabriel tiene un (**pedazo**, **trozo**, **cachito**) de coche.

11. Hoy no tengo ganas de (**currar**, **corrar**, **carrar**). Estoy enfermo.

12. Si sigues así, vas a cabar en el (**taladro**, **talego**, **talindro**).

ANSWERS TO LESSONS 1-10

LECCIÓN UNO - Hoy, tropecé con Maria en la calle.

(I ran into Maria in the street today.)

Practice the Vocabulary

A. 1. tropecé
2. enrolla
3. platicar
4. Caramba
5. chocante
6. donnadie
7. chusma
8. nena
9. latón
10. guay
11. evaporarme
12. enano

B. 1. donnadie
2. evaporarme
3. tropecé con
4. gentío
5. alucinaste
6. chusma
7. chismear
8. chocante
9. guay
10. platicar
11. chulear
12. latón

C. 1. L
2. E
3. A
4. B
5. C
6. D
7. G
8. F
9. H
10. K
11. J
12. I

D. **CROSSWORD PUZZLE**

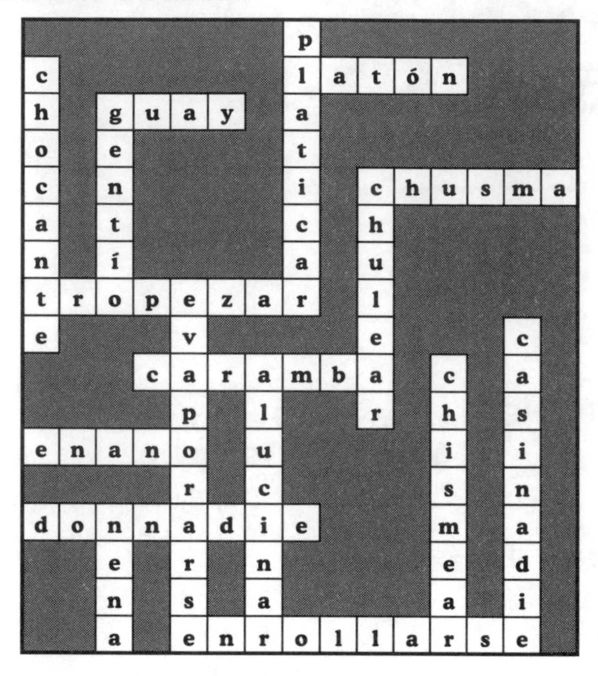

LECCIÓN DOS - ¡Yo creo que Juan se ha chupado demasiadas chelas!

(I think Juan drank a few too many beers!)

Practice the Vocabulary

A. 1. Parece que Jorge está bebido.
2. Ese tipo está cuadrado
3. Pedro tiene la bocaza muy grande.
4. Esa mujer está buenona.
5. Quiero ir a la pachanga de Juan.
6. Ese hombre es un gafudo.
7. Javier es muy empollón.
8. Marta es una foca.
9. Marisol está de gala esta noche.
10. Antonio fuma demasiados pitillos.
11. A Marco le gusta chupar demasiado.
12. Ese tipo es un cachas.

B. 1. cruda
2. buenona
3. colarse
4. gafudo
5. chelas
6. jeta
7. bocaza
8. tío
9. cachas
10. foca
11. empollón
12. piropos

C. 1. a
2. b
3. b
4. b
5. a
6. b
7. a
8. a
9. a
10. b
11. b
12. a

D. **DIALOGUE**

Ricardo: Mira quien acaba de **colarse** en el bar...Teresa Lopez. Oye, esta noche está **de gala**. ¡Es una verdadera **buenona**!

Adriana: Estoy segura de que le gustaría el **piropo**. Dime, ¿Conoces a ese **tío** con el **pitillo** en la **bocaza**?

Ricardo: ¿Te refieres al **gafudo** que está al lado de la **foca**? Nunca le había visto antes.

Adriana: Es Juan Valdez. Me sorprende verlo en esta **pachanga**. Solía ser un **empollón** pero de repente se ha convertido en un **cachas**. ¡Qué **jeta**! ¡Y además está **cuadrado**!

Ricardo: Yo creo que se ha **chupado** demasiadas **chelas**. Me parece que está **bebido**. ¡No me sorprendería nada si se levanta mañana con una **cruda**!

E. **FIND-A-WORD SPHERE**

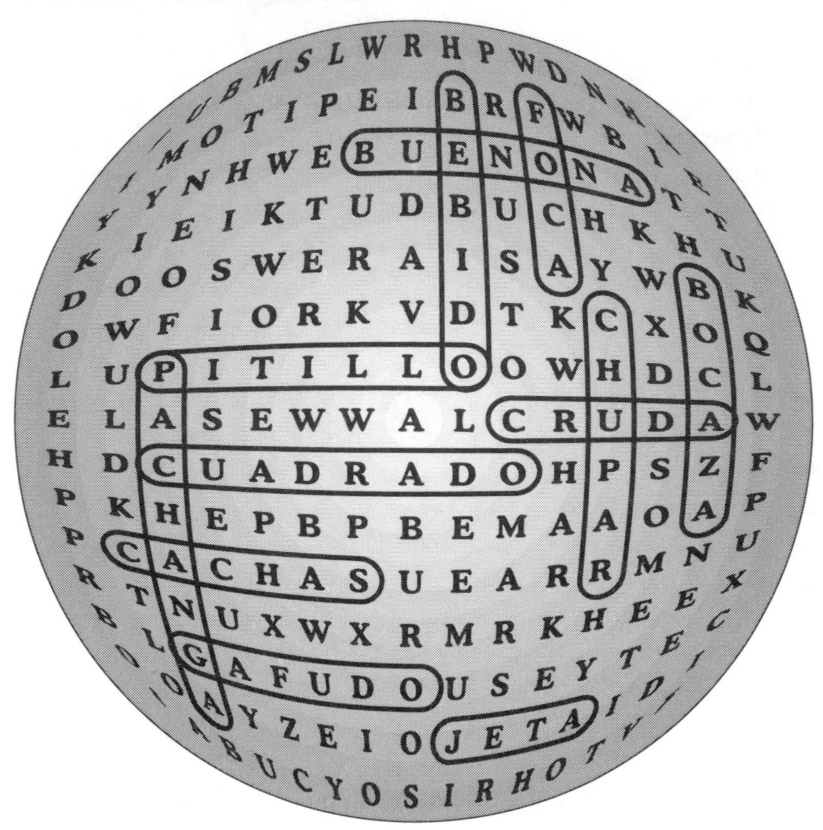

LECCIÓN TRES - Alfonso es un pez gordo en su compañía.

(Alfonso is a big wig at his company.)

Practice the Vocabulary

A.
1. gazpacho
2. colmo
3. en ascuas
4. pez gordo
5. trastornado
6. enchufe
7. fichado
8. currar
9. poli
10. chorrada
11. lana
12. besugo

B. 1. D
2. E
3. J
4. G
5. K
6. C
7. L
8. F
9. B
10. H
11. I
12. A

C. **CROSSWORD PUZZLE**

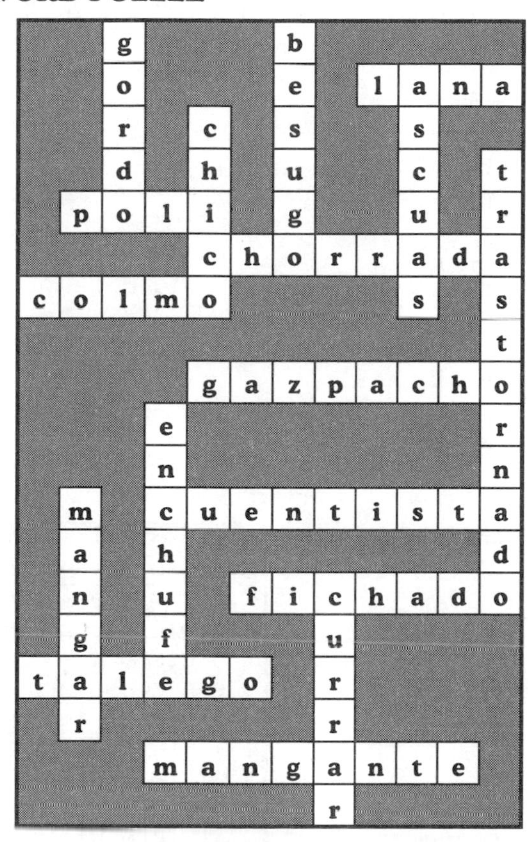

D. 1. besugo
2. cuentista
3. currar
4. colmo
5. enchufe
6. poli
7. talego
8. lana
9. gazpacho
10. trastornado
11. pez gordo
12. chico

LECCIÓN CUATRO - Mi media naranja y yo estamos celebrando nuestro aniversario.

(My wife and I are celebrating our anniversary.)

Practice the Vocabulary

A. 1. b
2. b
3. a
4. b
5. b
6. a
7. b
8. b
9. a
10. b
11. b
12. a

B. 1. c
2. b
3. a
4. c
5. c
6. a
7. b
8. c
9. b
10. a
11. b
12. c

C. 1. D
2. H
3. I
4. J
5. C
6. A
7. B
8. F
9. G
10. E
11. L
12. K

D. **FIND-A-WORD PUZZLE**

D S Y O N A E A T J W E
O A G O T A D O O A A S
N T J M E D S U M D S M
D O O A M U E R M A D O
A U U S Q K N C N T E R
J C R C U E N T Ó N R R
V H S H E E A A H S C O
I A D O S L R N E C H C
E M E M P L A T A A E O
J B J B A A N R U R N T
O E E R N H J C H D N U
S A V E S E A E K E O D
Q R A A M H R L N S C O
C T I U L T E S U W H C
V A S S N E C E E I O U
B U I T R E H E V L R A
H R V E I S U I O L R T
U E A P T I L T L W A E
C H O L L O O H Y O A O

LECCIÓN CINCO - ¡Esta chica es un verdadero merengue!

(That girl's a real babe!)

Practice the Vocabulary

A. 1. arregla
2. adoquín
3. mugre
4. Hombre
5. trupe
6. comecocos
7. chulada
8. escuincles
9. comerme el coco
10. merengue
11. contado
12. tertulia

B. 1. comecocos
2. Hombre
3. arreglas
4. chulada
5. adoquín
6. chunga
7. coco
8. trupe
9. tertulia
10. mugre
11. al contado
12. escuincles

C. 1. D
2. F
3. L
4. G
5. H
6. K
7. I
8. E
9. J
10. B
11. C
12. A

D. **DIALOGUE**

Esperanza: ¡**Hombre**! Cuando te **arreglas** te ves bellísima. Los chicos van a pensar que eres un verdadero **merengue** cuando te vean en la **tertulia** de esta noche. Espero que no creas que soy un **comecocos**, pero ese vestido es una **chulada**. Es mucho más bonito que el vestido que te pusiste antes. Parecías un **escuincle**.

Irene: Tienes razón. Pero este me encanta. De hecho, creo que también voy a comprar el bolso y los zapatos que van con este vestido. No quiero venir con toda la **trupe**, así que voy a comprarlos ahora y voy a **pagar al contado**. Espero que no me toque ese **adoquín** y me derrame salsa de tomate o algo encima.

Esperanza: No **te comas el coco** tanto. Además, si ves que tiene un poquito de **mugre**, lo puedes lavar.

ANSWERS TO REVIEW EXAM FOR LESSONS 1-5

A. 1. a
2. b
3. b
4. b
5. b
6. b
7. a
8. b
9. a
10. a
11. b
12. b
13. a
14. b
15. a
16. a
17. b
18. a
19. b
20. a
21. b
22. b
23. a

B. 1. colmo
2. chulada
3. chambear
4. suertudo
5. ascuas
6. buenona
7. trupe
8. chollo
9. adoquín
10. chelas
11. tertulia
12. chismear

C. 1. G
2. A
3. L
4. B
5. K
6. J
7. D
8. E
9. F
10. I
11. C
12. H

D. 1. caramba
2. donnadie
3. enano
4. bocaza
5. pachanga
6. cachas
7. foca
8. lana
9. colmo
10. amuermado
11. viejos
12. comecocos

LECCIÓN SEIS - Parece que mi nueva vecina tiene una caradura increíble.

(My new neighbor seems like a real arrogant person.)

Practice the Vocabulary

A. 1. manitas
2. montón
3. raro
4. antenas
5. carroza
6. coco
7. pesado
8. corte
9. flote
10. cuatroojos
11. horripilante
12. renacuajos

B.
1. caradura
2. caramelo
3. cochazo
4. conocí
5. largarme
6. pila
7. manitas
8. horripilante
9. montón
10. renacuajo
11. cuatroojos
12. raro

C.
1. D
2. F
3. E
4. I
5. C
6. G
7. K
8. L
9. J
10. B
11. H
12. A

D. **CROSSWORD PUZZLE**

LECCIÓN SIETE - Mira ese jugador narizón. ¡Qué ardilla!

(Look at that guy with the big honker. What a smart cookie!)

Practice the Vocabulary

A. 1. a
2. b
3. a
4. a
5. b
6. b
7. b
8. a
9. b
10. a
11. a
12. b

B. 1. son como
2. malísimamente
3. ardilla
4. Qué va
5. verme
6. narizón
7. bólido
8. vacilando
9. chungo
10. regatear
11. bailón
12. chupón

C. 1. D
2. H
3. E
4. G
5. K
6. L
7. J
8. I
9. F
10. C
11. A
12. B

D. **FIND-A-WORD PUZZLE**

M	B	R	T	I	M	E	L	M	N	G	W
T	A	L	E	G	C	H	U	P	Ó	N	T
M	I	D	O	W	O	C	E	U	W	Z	R
A	L	A	L	A	M	H	M	R	A	P	A
B	Ó	L	I	D	O	U	U	T	I	A	S
C	N	A	J	A	A	F	R	I	L	V	T
U	E	O	A	M	I	G	U	E	T	E	O
V	M	L	A	A	T	M	O	M	Y	R	R
A	R	D	I	L	L	A	L	P	M	S	N
Y	R	C	T	Í	O	S	I	O	E	E	A
A	P	U	E	S	B	E	S	U	V	O	D
H	N	A	R	I	Z	Ó	N	O	A	R	O
U	C	N	R	M	Y	F	E	N	C	D	H
C	A	C	H	A	R	R	O	S	I	O	O
H	L	I	U	M	U	C	S	E	L	M	W
U	M	S	R	E	G	A	T	E	A	R	A
N	O	T	N	N	M	A	N	G	R	R	S
G	O	L	I	T	A	D	V	M	M	M	T
O	Y	M	M	E	N	E	A	R	S	E	A

LECCIÓN OCHO - ¡Qué burro!

(What a jerk!)

Practice the Vocabulary

A.
1. a
2. b
3. a
4. b
5. a
6. b
7. a
8. b
9. a
10. b
11. b
12. a

B.
1. burro
2. correr
3. desmadre
4. domingueros
5. lata
6. pinchó
7. regalito
8. rollo
9. romper a
10. vivo
11. allá
12. azotea

C.
1. burro
2. cacharritos
3. chamacos
4. azotea
5. lata
6. Olé
7. domingueros
8. desmadre
9. colarse
10. viva
11. rollo
12. romper

D. **DIALOGUE**

Anabel: ¿Cuando vamos a llegar? Yo no tenía ni idea que la feria estaba tan **allá**.

Marcelo: Quisiera poder **correr** más, pero lo que pasa es que hay muchos **domingueros** en la carretera. Ya sabes, la última vez que fui a la feria tardé seis horas porque me dieron un **regalito**...¡**se me pinchó una llanta**!

Anabel: ¡Qué **lata**!

Marcelo: ¡Creí que iba a **romper a** llorar! Yo creía que era lo bastante **vivo** como para cambiar la llanta, así que lo hice yo mismo. Pero mientras estaba cambiándola, me dieron un **leñazo** en la **azotea** porque un **burro** me tiró una lata de soda desde su bólido. ¡Qué **desmadre**! ¡Me enojé tanto!

Anabel: ¡Qué **rollo**! Bueno, yo no creo que tengas que preocuparte de eso esta vez porque ¡la feria está allí mismo!

Marcelo: ¡**Olé**! Espero que no haya desmasiados **chamacos**. El año pasado se **colaban** en todos los **cacharritos** más divertidos.

LECCIÓN NUEVE - Esta tía está bien conservada para su edad.

(This woman looks well preserved for her age.)

Practice the Vocabulary

A. 1. a
2. b
3. b
4. a
5. a
6. b
7. a
8. a
9. b
10. a
11. a
12. a

B.
1. charlar
2. huevón
3. dulzura
4. bueno
5. conservado
6. barbas
7. testarudo
8. liado
9. tía
10. rollo
11. follón
12. se trata

C.
1. J
2. L
3. K
4. A
5. I
6. D
7. H
8. F
9. G
10. E
11. C
12. B

D. **FIND-A-WORD CUBE**

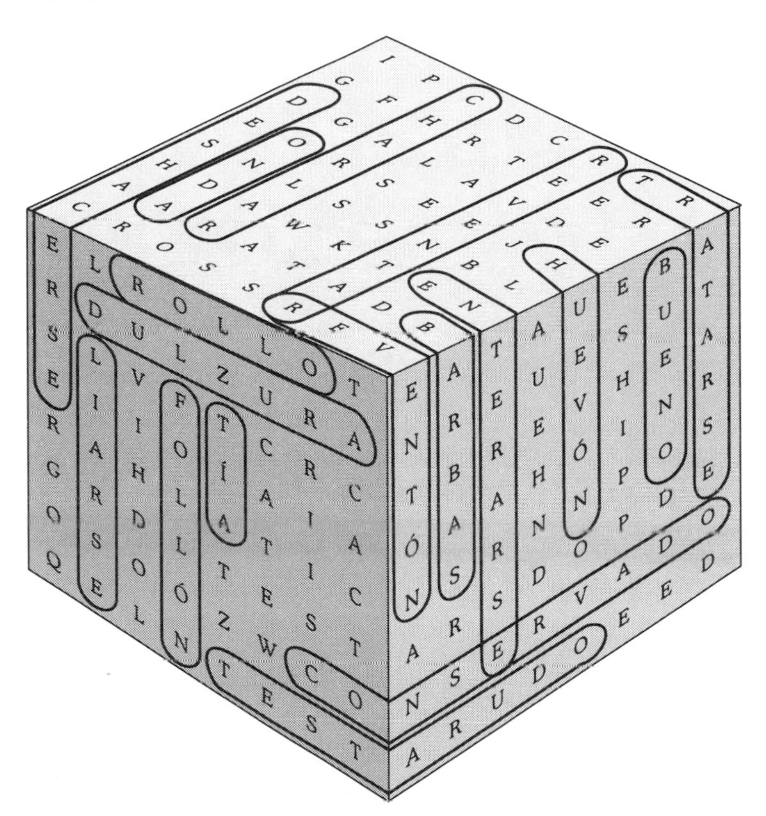

LECCIÓN DIEZ - ¡Ese tío tiene mucha pasta!

(This guy has a lot of money!)

Practice the Vocabulary

A.
1. aguafiestas
2. gozador
3. matasanos
4. robot
5. galán
6. cita sorpresa
7. pavor
8. pasta
9. supercontento
10. bravo
11. canijo
12. tragar

B.
1. a
2. b
3. a
4. b
5. a
6. b
7. a
8. a
9. a
10. b
11. a
12. b

C.
1. bobo
2. callejear
3. castillo
4. supercontento
5. cita sorpresa
6. creído
7. galán
8. gozador
9. matasanos
10. pedazo
11. plata
12. tragar

D. CROSSWORD PUZZLE

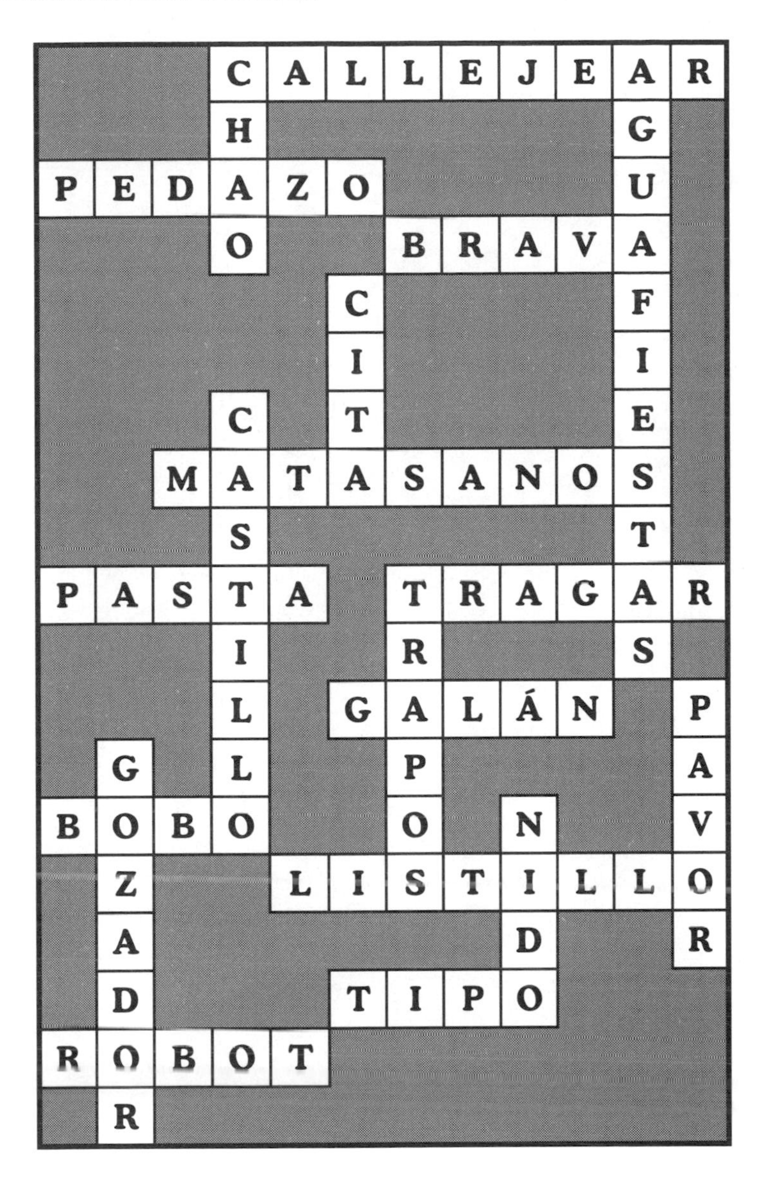

ANSWERS TO REVIEW EXAM FOR LESSONS 6-10

A.
1. b
2. a
3. a
4. a
5. a
6. b
7. b
8. a
9. a
10. a
11. a
12. a
13. a
14. a
15. b
16. a
17. a
18. b
19. a
20. a
21. b
22. b
23. b

B.
1. gordinflón
2. aguafiestas
3. domingueros
4. narizón
5. manitas
6. rollo
7. carroza
8. reventón
9. renacuajos
10. lija
11. leñazo
12. gozador

C.
1. G
2. I
3. K
4. H
5. L
6. J
7. C
8. E
9. D
10. B
11. F
12. A

D.
1. nido
2. pila
3. bailón
4. metió
5. desmadre
6. lata
7. barbas
8. tía
9. canijo
10. pedazo
11. currar
12. talego

APPENDIX

-Dictations-

Lección Uno

Hoy, tropecé con María en la calle.
(I ran into Maria in the street today.)

1. Hoy, **tropecé** con María en la calle.
2. Me detuve a **platicar** con ella.
3. No soporto a esa **nena**.
4. Deberías de haber intentado **evaporarte** en el **gentío**.
5. Es que es tan **chocante**.
6. Siempre está **chuleando**.
7. ¡Qué **guay**!
8. Todo lo que hizo esta vez fue **chismear** sobre Jorge.

Lección Dos

¡Yo creo que Juan se ha chupado demasiadas chelas!
(I think Juan drank a few too many beers!)

1. Mira quien acaba de **colarse**.
2. Oye, esta noche está **de gala**.
3. ¡Es una verdadera **buenona**!
4. ¿Conoces a ese **tío** con el **pitillo** en la **bocaza**?
5. ¿Te refieres al **gafudo** que está al lado de la **foca**?
6. Me sorprende verlo en esta **pachanga**.
7. Solía ser un **empollón**.
8. ¡Qué **jeta**!

Lección Tres

Alfonso es un pez gordo en su compañía.

(Alfonso is a big wig in his company.)

1. ¡Estoy **en ascuas**!
2. El jefe acusó a Ricardo de **mangar** de la compañía.
3. Cuando el **pez gordo** lo averiguó, hasta llamó a la **poli**.
4. Ricardo gana mucha **lana**.
5. Siempre me ha parecido un **chico** muy decente.
6. ¡Qué **gazpacho**!
7. Ya estaba **fichado** por el jefe.
8. ¡Esto es **el colmo**!

Lección Cuatro

Mi media naranja y yo estamos celebrando nuestro aniversario.

(My wife and I are celebrating our anniversary.)

1. ¡Oye mi **cuate**!
2. ¿**Qué hay de nuevo**?
3. Pareces **amuermado** hoy.
4. Estoy **agotado** porque he tenido que **chambear** tarde toda la semana.
5. ¡Qué **rechulo**!
6. ¡Eso si que es un regalo **morrocotudo**!
7. Espero que sepa lo **suertuda** que es de tener un **hombre** como tú.
8. Voy a pagar tu **cuentón**.

Lección Cinco

¡Esta chica es un verdadero merengue!

(That girl's a real babe!)

1. Cuando te **arreglas** te ves bellísima.
2. Los chicos van a pensar que eres un verdadero **merengue**.
3. Espero que no creas que soy un **comecocos**.
4. Ese era muy **chungo**.
5. Parecías un **escuincle**.
6. No quiero venir con toda la **trupe**.
7. Voy a **pagar al contado**.
8. No te **comas el coco** tanto.

Lección Seis

Parece que mi nueva vecina tiene una caradura increíble.

(My new neighbor seems like a real arrogant person.)

1. Hoy **conocí** a los nuevos vecinos.
2. Me dieron un **corte**.
3. Son muy **raros**.
4. **Me largué** en seguida.
5. Es una **carroza**.
6. Tiene una **caradura** increíble.
7. Es un **cuatrojos** con el **coco** muy pequeño.
8. Me da la impresíon de que tienen un **montón** de **renacuajos**.

Lección Siete

Mira ese jugador narizón. ¡Qué ardilla!
(Look at that guy with the big honker. What a smart cookie!)

1. ¡**Vaya**!, ¡mi **amiguete**!
2. Voy a **verme con** Julio.
3. Nunca **se presenta a tiempo**.
4. Su **bólido** siempre tiene alguna avería.
5. Es un verdadero **cacharro**.
6. Ahora **son como** las dos de la tarde.
7. ¿Te refieres al jugador **narizón**?
8. Yo creo que ese tío es una **ardilla**.

Lección Ocho

¡Qué burro!
(What a jerk!)

1. Yo no tenía ni idea que la feria estaba tan **allá**.
2. Quisiera poder **correr** más.
3. Hay muchos **domingueros** en la carretera.
4. ¡Qué **lata**!
5. ¡Creí que iba a **romper a** llorar!
6. Un **burro** me tiró una lata de soda desde su **bólido**.
7. ¡Qué **desmandre**!
8. Espero que no haya desmasiados **chamacos**.

Lección Nueve

Esta tía está bien conservada para su edad.

(This woman looks well preserved for her age.)

1. Espero que el **rollo** empiece pronto.
2. **Me revienta** cuando empiezan tarde.
3. ¿Te **enteraste** de qué **se trata** el rollo?
4. Se trata de una **tía** que tiene cincuenta **abriles**.
5. Unos meses más tarde **se lía** con el **tío**.
6. No es tan **buena onda** como todo el mundo cree.
7. Enrique es un **testarudo** y un **huevón**.
8. Ella no sabe como **deshacerse de** él.

Lección Diez

¡Ese tío tiene mucha pasta!

(This guy has a lot of money!)

1. ¡Pareces que estás **brava** hoy!
2. ¿No te lo pasaste bien anoche en tu **cita sorpresa**?
3. Marco vino a mi **nido** a eso de las ocho de la noche.
4. Yo **tenía pavor** de que iba a ser un **bobo** o un **gordinflón**.
5. Es un verdadero **galán**.
6. Al ver su auto y sus **trapos**, se veía que era un gran **gozador**.
7. Le pregunté que si quería algo de **tragar**.
8. ¡Qué tipo más **aguafiestas**!

Glossary

a que *exp.* I'll bet (you) • (lit.): to that.

example: **A que** llueve el día de mi cumpleaños.

translation: **I'll bet you** it rains on my birthday.

abriles (tener ____) *exp.* to be ____ years old • (lit.): to have____ Aprils.

example: Lola es tan joven. Sólo **tiene 20 abriles**.

translation: Lola is so young. She's only **20 years old**.

ALSO -1: **tener muchas millas** *exp.* to be very old • (lit.): to have many miles.

NOTE: This expression is usually used in reference to an old woman.

ALSO -2: **tener ____ años y muchos meses** *exp.* to be old • (lit.): to be ____ years old and many months more.

SYNONYM: **primaveras (tener ____)** *exp. (Mexico)* • (lit.): to have ____ springtimes.

adoquín *m.* jerk, fool, moron, simpleton • (lit.): paving block.

example: Julio es un **adoquín**. Siempre está diciendo estupideces.

translation: Julio is a **jerk**. He's always talking nonsense.

SYNONYM -1: **boludo** *m. (Argentina)*.

SYNONYM -2: **bruto/a** *adj.* • (lit.): stupid, crude.

SYNONYM -3: **caballo** *m. (Puerto Rico)*.

SYNONYM -4: **cabezota** *adj.*

NOTE: This comes from the feminine noun *cabeza* meaning "head." The suffix *ota* is commonly used to modify the meaning of a noun; in this case, changing it to "big head."

SYNONYM -5: **cateto/a** *adj. (Spain)*.

SYNONYM -6: **chorlito** *m.* • (lit.): golden plover (which is a kind of bird).

SYNONYM -7: **goma** *f. (Argentina)* • (lit.): rubber, glue.

SYNONYM -8: **matado/a** *n. (Spain)* idiot or nerd.

SYNONYM -9: **menso/a** *n. (Mexico)*.

SYNONYM -10: **pendejo** *m. (Argentina)* • **1.** idiot, imbecile • **2.** coward • (lit.): public hair.

SYNONYM -11: **soquete** *m. (Cuba)*.

SYNONYM -12: **tarado/a** *adj.* *(Argentina).*

SYNONYM -13: **tosco/a** *adj.* • (lit.): coarse, crude, unrefined.

SYNONYM -14: **zopenco/a** *adj.* • (lit.): dull, stupid.

ANTONYM -1: **avispado/a** *adj.* • (lit.): clever, sharp.

NOTE: This comes from the term *avispa* meaning "wasp."

ANTONYM -2: **despabilado/a** *adj.* • (lit.): awakened.

NOTE: This comes from the verb *despavilar* meaning "to wake up."

ANTONYM -3: **despejado/a** *adj.* • (lit.): confident, assured (in behavior), clear (as in a cloudless sky).

ANTONYM -4: **listillo/a** *adj.* • (lit.): a small clever person.

NOTE: This comes from the adjective *listo/a* meaning "ready" or "clever."

ANTONYM -5: **pillo** *adj.* • (lit.): roguish, mischievous.

NOTE: This adjective is always used in the masculine form. Interestingly enough, the feminine form, *pilla*, is rarely ever seen.

ANTONYM -6: **vivo/a** *adj.* • (lit.): alive.

agotado/a (estar) *adj.* to be exhausted, completely tired out • (lit.): to be emptied or drained.

example: He trabajado toda la noche. Estoy **agotado**.

translation: I worked all night long. I'm **pooped**.

SYNONYM -1: **como un trapo viejo (estar / sentirse)** *exp.* • (lit.): to be/to feel like an old rag.

SYNONYM -2: **hecho polvo (estar)** *exp.* • (lit.): to be made of dust.

SYNONYM -3: **muerto/a (estar)** *adj.* • (lit.): to be dead.

SYNONYM -4: **rendido/a (estar)** *adj.* • (lit.): to be rendered (all off one's energy).

SYNONYM -5: **reventado/a (estar)** *adj.* • (lit.): to be burst (like a balloon whose air has been suddenly let out).

aguafiestas *m.* party-pooper, stick in the mud, kill-joy • (lit.): water-festival (referring to someone who "throws water on a festival" as one would throw on a fire to extinguish it).

example: A mi novio no le gusta ir a bailar. ¡Es un verdadero **aguafiestas**!

translation: My boyfriend never likes to go out dancing. He's such a **stick in the mud**!

SYNONYM -1: **aguado/a** *n.* *(Mexico).*

SYNONYM -2: **chocante** *m.* *(Mexico).*

SYNONYM -3: **embolante** *m.* *(Argentina).*

allá (estar tan) *exp.* to be very far away • (lit.): to be so there.

example: ¡Yo no sabía que Chicago **estaba tan allá**!

translation: I didn't know Chicago was **so far away**!

ALSO: **muy allá** *exp.* very far away • (lit.): very there.

alucinar *v.* to amaze, to astonish, to hallucinate.

example: Me **alucinaste** cuando te presentaste en la fiesta en bikini.

translation: You **astonished** me when you showed up at the party wearing a bikini.

SYNONYM -1: **eslembar** *v. (Puerto Rico / Cuba).*

SYNONYM -2: **flipar** *v. (Spain).*

amiguete *m. (Spain)* pal, buddy, friend.

example: Felipe es mi **amiguete**. Siempre puedo contar con él.

translation: Felipe is my **pal**. I can always count on him.

VARIATION: **amigote** *m.*

NOTE: **amiguete del alma** *exp.* bosom buddy, close friend • (lit.): buddy of the soul.

SYNONYM -1: **colega** *m. (Spain)* • (lit.): colleague.

SYNONYM -2: **cuate** *m. (Mexico)* pal, buddy.

SYNONYM -3: **tronco** *m. (Argentina)* • (lit.): truck (of a tree).

amuermado/a (estar) *adj.* to be out of it, dazed.

example: Parece que Luis no durmió bien anoche. Hoy está **amuermado**.

translation: It looks like Luis didn't sleep well last night. He's **out of it** today.

SYNONYM -1: **aplantanado/a** *adj.*

SYNONYM -2: **aturdido/a** *adj.*

SYNONYM -3: **volando/a** *adj. (Argentina).*

antenas *f.pl. (Spain)* • (lit.): antennas.

example: Manolo tiene las **antenas** tan grandes que parece un elefante.

translation: Manolo has such **big ears** he looks like an elephant.

NOTE: **orejudo/a** *adj.* big-eared (from the feminine noun *oreja* meaning "ear").

SYNONYM: **guatacas** *f.pl. (Cuba).*

aparecer a tiempo *exp.* to arrive on time • to appear on time.

example: Mi maestro de matemáticas siempre **aparece a tiempo**.

translation: My math teacher always **shows up on time**.

SYNONYM: **llagar a tiempo** *exp.* • (lit.): to arrive on time.

ardilla *adj.* smart, bright, sharp • (lit.): squirrel.

example: Linda sabe mucho de computadoras. Es una verdadera **ardilla**.

translation: Linda knows a lot about computers. She's really **bright**.

SYNONYM -1: **águila** *m. (Cuba)* • (lit.): eagle.

SYNONYM -2: **listillo/a** *adj. (Spain).*

NOTE: This comes from the adjective *listo* meaning "clear" or "smart."

SYNONYM -3: **piola** *f. (Argentina)* a smart and clever person.

SYNONYM -4: **zorra** *f. (Puerto Rico)* • (lit.): fox.

ANTONYM: **burro/a** *adj.* dumb, stupid • (lit.): donkey – SEE: *p. 201*.

arreglarse *v.* to fix oneself up, to make oneself look attractive • (lit.): to fix oneself up (from the verb *arreglar* meaning "to repair something").

example: María está guapísima cuando **se arregla**.

translation: Maria is beautiful when she **fixes herself up**.

ALSO -1: **arreglarse con** *exp.* to conform to, to agree with, to come to an agreement with.

ALSO -2: **arreglárselas** *v.* to manage.

SYNONYM -1: **empaquetarse** *v. (Puerto Rico).*

SYNONYM -2: **pintarse** *v.* • (lit.): to paint oneself.

ascuas (estar en) *exp.* to be on pins and needles.

example: Estoy **en ascuas**. ¡No sé si voy a pasar el examen de matemáticas!

translation: I'm **on pins and needles**. I don't know if I'm going to pass the math test!

SYNONYM -1: **bolas (estar en)** *exp. (Argentina)* • (lit.): to be in balls (perhaps since one's hands may be clenched during times of great anticipation).

SYNONYM -2: **loco/a por saber algo (estar)** *exp. (Cuba)* • (lit.): to be crazy to know something.

azotea *f.* head • (lit.): flat or terraced roof.

example: ¡Caramba! Parece que este tío está mal de la **azotea.**

translation: Geez! I think that guy is **crazy**.

SYNONYMS: SEE - **coco**, *p. 207.*

bailón *m. (Spain)* dancer (usually applies to a Spanish folk dancer).

example: Andrés conoce a muchas chicas porque es un gran **bailón** y siempre va a las discotecas.

translation: Andrés knows a lot of girls because he's a great **dancer** and goes to discos al the time.

NOTE: This comes from the verb *bailar* meaning "to dance."

SYNONYM: **bailador/a** *n. (Spain).*

barbas *m.* bearded man.

example: Augusto siempre ha sido un **barbas**. Parece que no le gusta afeitarse.

translation: Augusto has always been a **bearded man**. It seems like he doesn't like to shave.

SYNONYM -1: **barbado** *m. (Puerto Rico).*

SYNONYM -2: **barbón** *m.*

SYNONYM -3: **barbudo** *m.*

NOTE: These synonyms come from the feminine noun *barba* meaning "beard."

SYNONYM -4: **fulano** *m. (Mexico).*

bebido/a (estar) *adj.* to be drunk, "wasted," inebriated.

example: Creo que Pedro está **bebido** porque no se puede mantener en pie.

translation: I think Pedro is **wasted** because he can't even stand up.

SYNONYM -1: **alegre (estar)** *adj.* • (lit.): to be happy.

SYNONYM -2: **borrachín (estar)** *adj.*

NOTE: This comes from the adjective *borracho/a* meaning "drunk."

SYNONYM -3: **cuba (estar)** *adj.*

SYNONYM -4: **en pedo** *adj.* *(Argentina)* • (lit.): in fart.

SYNONYM -5: **pellejo (estar)** *adj.* • (lit.): to be skin (as in chicken skin).

SYNONYM -6: **piripi (estar)** *adj.*

SYNONYM -7: **tomado/a (estar)** *adj.* • (lit.): to be drunk/taken.

besugo *m.* idiot, fool, harebrained person, scatterbrain • (lit.): sea bream (which is a kind of fish).

example: Jorge es un **besugo**. Siempre comete errores.

translation: Jorge is an **idiot**. He's always making mistakes.

SYNONYMS: SEE - **adoquín**, *p. 195.*

bien conservado/a (estar) *adj.* to be in good shape for one's age • (lit.): to be well preserved.

example: Julio está muy **bien conservado** para su edad.

translation: Julio is **well preserved** for his age.

VARIATION: **buena conservado/a (estar)** *adj.* *(Argentina)*

SYNONYM: **buena forma (estar en)** *exp.* • (lit.): to be in good form.

bobo/a *n.* idiot, fool.

example: Carlos es un **bobo**. No sabe ni atarse los cordones de los zapatos.

translation: Carlos is an **idiot**. He doesn't even know how to tie his shoes.

VARIATION: **bobo de capirote** *exp.* a complete idiot • (lit.): stupid in the hat.

SYNONYM -1: **asno** *adj.* • (lit.): donkey.

SYNONYM -2: **atontado/a** *adj.* • (lit.): stupid person.

SYNONYM -3: **bobazo** *m.* *(Argentina).*

SYNONYM -4: **burro** *adj.* • (lit.): donkey – SEE: *burro, p. 201.*

SYNONYM -5: **ganso** *adj.* • (lit.): goose.

SYNONYM -6: **mentecato/a** *adj.* • (lit.): silly, foolish.

SYNONYM -7: **pasmarote** *adj.* • (lit.): silly, foolish.

SYNONYM -8: **patoso/a** *adj.* • (lit.): boring, dull.

SYNONYM -9: **tonto/a** *adj.* • (lit.): stupid person.

SYNONYM -10: **zopenco/a** *adj.* • (lit.): dull, stupid.

SYNONYM -11: **zoquete** *adj.* • (lit.): chump, block (of wood).

ANTONYM -1: **listillo/a** *adj.* *(Spain)* • (lit.): small clever person.

ANTONYM -2: **pillo** *adj.* • (lit.): roguish, mischievous, rascally.

ANTONYM -3: **vivo/a** *adj.* clever, smart • (lit.): alive.

bocaza *f.* mouth, big mouth.

example: ¡Ese tipo tiene la **bocaza** tan grande como la de un tiburón!

translation: That guy's **mouth** is as big as a shark's!

SYNONYM: **bocacha** *f.*

bólido *m. (Spain)* car, automobile • (lit.): race car.

example: Ana y yo vamos a dar una vuelta en mi **bólido** nuevo.

translation: Ana and I are going for a ride in my new **car**.

NOTE: In formal Spanish, this term usually refers to a great car, although it occasionally used in a sarcastic way referring to a car that does not work properly.

SYNONYM -1: **autazo** *m. (Argentina).*

SYNONYM -2: **auto** *m. (Argentina).*

SYNONYM -3: **buga** *f. (Spain).*

SYNONYM -4: **carrazo** *m. (Puerto Rico / Cuba)* big car.

SYNONYM -5: **cochazo** *m.*

SYNONYM -6: **coche** *m. (Argentina).*

SYNONYM -7: **carro** *m. (Mexico / Cuba).*

SYNONYM -8: **máquina** *f. (Puerto Rico)* machine.

bravo/a *adj.* upset, angry • (lit.): fierce, ferocious.

example: Lucía está **brava** hoy porque no durmió bien anoche.

translation: Lucia is **upset** today because she didn't sleep well last night.

ALSO: ¡**Bravo**! *interj.* Well done!

SYNONYM -1: **cabreado/a** *adj. (Spain).*

SYNONYM -2: **embolado/a** *adj. (Argentina).*

buena onda *f.* good egg, good person • (lit.): good wave.

example: Agustín es muy **buena onda**. Siempre está dispuesto a ayudar.

translation: Agustín is a **good egg**. He is always willing to help.

SYNONYM -1: **buena gente** *f.* good person • (lit.): good people.

NOTE: The term *buena gente* is commonly used to refer to only one person, although the literal translation is indeed plural. However, when used to refer to a group of people, it is no longer considered slang rather academic Spanish.

SYNONYM -2: **buenas (estar de)** *adj. (Puerto Rico).*

SYNONYM -3: **buen partido / buena partida** *n. (Cuba).*

SYNONYM -4: **tío enrollado** *m. (Spain)* • (lit.): rolled up uncle (or a person rolled up into one great package).

NOTE: **tío** *m. (Cuba / Spain)* man, "dude."

bueno/a • **1.** *adj.* well... • **2.** *interj.* sure! • **3.** *adj.* bad, nasty • **4.** *adj.* considerable • **5.** *interj.* come off it! • **6.** *adj.* okay • (lit.): good.

example (1): **Bueno**, resulta que Alvaro y Fiona se van de vacaciones a Paris.

translation: **Well**, it so happens that Alvaro and Fiona are going on vacation to Paris.

example (2): ¿Quieres comer en ese restaurante?
¡**Bueno**!

translation: Do you want to eat in that restaurant?
Sure!

example (3): Me siento muy mal. Tengo un **buen** costipado.

translation: I feel sick. I have a **very bad** cold.

example (4): Parece que José tiene una **buena** cantidad de dinero en el banco.

translation: It seems that Jose has a **considerable** amount of money in the bank.

example (5): ¡Me acabo de enterar que mis antepasados eran nobles!
¡**Bueno**! Eso es un poco difícil de creer.

translation: I just found out that my ancestors are royalty!
Come off it! That's a little hard to believe.

example (6): ¿Te gustó la película de anoche?
Bueno. Me gustó más o menos.

translation: Did you like the movie last night?
It was okay. I sort of liked it.

NOTE: In Mexico, using the interjection *bueno* is a common way of answering the telephone.

SYNONYM: **caramba** *interj. (Puerto Rico)* used as a synonym for definition **1**.

buenona *f.* beautiful woman, a knockout.

example: La profesora nueva de matemáticas es una verdadera **buenona**.

translation: The new math teacher is a real **knockout**.

SYNONYM -1: **buenachón** *f. (Puerto Rico).*

SYNONYM -2: **cuero** *m.* • (lit.): skin.

SYNONYM -3: **diosa** *f. (Argentina)* • (lit.): goddess.

SYNONYM -4: **potra** *f. (Argentina).*

SYNONYM -5: **tía buena** *f. (Spain / Cuba)* • (lit.): aunt good.

buitre *m.* • **1.** cheapskate • **2.** opportunist • (lit.): vulture.

example (1): Jorge es tan **buitre** que nunca desayuna para ahorrar dinero.

translation: Jorge is such a **cheapskate** that he never eats breakfast just so that he can save money.

example (2): Julio es un **buitre**. Cuando perdí mi trabajo, en vez de ayudarme, intentó conseguir mi trabado.

translation: Julio is a real **opportunist**. When I lost my job, instead of helping me, he tried to get my old job.

SYNONYM: **amarrete** *m. (Argentina).*

burro *m.* jerk, fool, moron, simpleton, stupid person • (lit.): donkey.

example: José es un **burro**. Nunca hace nada bien.

translation: Jose is a **moron**. He never does anything right.

SYNONYMS: SEE - **adoquín**, *p. 195*.

cacharritos *m.pl.* rides in an amusement park • (lit.): small pieces of junk, small machines that don't work properly.

example: Cuando fuimos al parque de atracciones David y Stefani se subieron en todos los **cacharritos**.

translation: When we went to the amusement park, David and Stefani went on every **ride**.

NOTE: This is a very popular expression especially among kids.

cacharro *m.* • **1.** jalopy, old wreck • **2.** lemon (any piece of machinery that does not work properly).

example (1): Este **cacharro** nunca quiere arrancar por las mañanas.

translation: This **old wreck** never wants to start in the morning.

example (2): Este lavaplatos no limpia los platos bien. Es un **cacharro**.

translation: This dishwasher doesn't clean the dishes properly. It's a **piece of junk**.

SYNONYM: **porquería** *f. (Argentina)* said of anything worthless.

cachas *m.* good-looking young man, a hunk.

example: Sergio está haciendo mucho deporte últimamente. Se está convirtiendo en un **cachas**.

translation: Sergio is doing a lot of exercise lately. He's becoming a real **hunk**.

SYNONYM -1: **canchero** *m. (Argentina)* • (lit.): expert, skilled.

SYNONYM -2: **langa** *m. (Argentina)*.

NOTE: This is a reverse transformation of the word *galán* (lan-ga) meaning "gallant" or "handsome."

SYNONYM -3: **tío bueno** *m. (Cuba / Spain)* • (lit.): uncle good.

SYNONYM -4: **tofete** *m. (Puerto Rico)*.

SYNONYM -5: **tremendo tipazo** *m. (Cuba)*.

callejear *v.* to take a walk.

example: Cuando hace sol me gusta **callejear**.

translation: When it's sunny outside, I enjoy going for a **walk**.

SYNONYM: **dar una vuelta** *exp.*to go for a walk • (lit.): to give around.

canijo/a *adj.* • **1.** very skinny person • **2.** feeble, frail, sickly.

example: Ese tipo es un verdadero **canijo**. Parece que nunca come.

translation: That guy is **really skinny**. It looks like he never eats.

SYNONYM -1: **esqueleto** *m. (Puerto Rico / Cuba)*• (lit.): skeleton.

SYNONYM -2: **flacuyo** *adj. (Argentina)*.

caradura *f.* • **1.** arrogant • **2.** nervy, brazen • (lit.): hard face.

example (1): Pedro es un **caradura**. Se cree que es mejor que nadie.

translation: Pedro is so **arrogant**. He thinks he's better than anybody else.

example (2): Jose Luis es tan **caradura** que siempre le pide dinero a sus amigos.

translation: Jose Luis is so **nervy**. He's always asking his friends for money.

SYNONYM: **descarado/a** *adj.* • (lit.): faceless (from the feminine noun *cara* meaning "face").

caramba *interj.* geez, holy cow.

example: ¡**Caramba**!, no me puedo creer el calor que hace.

translation: **Geez**! I can't believe how warm it is.

SYNONYMS: SEE - **¡Hombre!**, *p. 216.*

caramelo *m.* beautiful woman, knockout, "fox" • (lit.): candy.

example: Anabel es un verdadero **caramelo**. Se nota que se cuida.

translation: Anabel is a real **fox**. You can tell she takes care of herself.

SYNONYMS: SEE - **merengue**, *p. 221.*

carroza *f.* elderly person, old relic • (lit.): carriage.

example: Esa mujer es una **carroza**. Parece que tiene noventa años.

translation: That woman is an **old relic**. She looks like she is ninety.

SYNONYM -1: **abuelo** *m.* • (lit.): grandfather.

SYNONYM -2: **añoso** *m.* • (lit.): from the masculine noun *año* meaning "year."

SYNONYM -3: **antañón** *m.* • (lit.): from the masculine noun *antaño* meaning "long ago."

SYNONYM -4: **Más viejo que Matusalén** *exp.* very old person • (lit.): older than Methuselah.

SYNONYM -5: **prehistórico** *m.* • (lit.): prehistoric.

SYNONYM -6: **reliquia histórica** *f. (Cuba)* • (lit.): historic relic.

SYNONYM -7: **vejestorio** *m.* • (lit.): from the adjective *viejo* meaning "old."

SYNONYM -8: **vejete** *m.* • (lit.): from the adjective *viejo* meaning "old."

casinadie *m.* a person of great integrity and influence, a very important person • (lit.): almost nobody.

example: ¡Mira! Por ahí viene el Señor Smith, es **casinadie** in esta compañía.

translation: Look! Here comes Mr. Smith. He's a **very important person** in this company.

ANTONYM: **donnadie** *m.* loser • (lit.): Mr. Nobody - SEE: *p. 212.*

castillo *m.* home, house • (lit.): castle.

example: ¿Te gusta mi **castillo** nuevo? Tiene cuatro dormitorios.

translation: Do you like my new **house**? It has four bedrooms.

SYNONYM -1: **hogar** *m.* • (lit.): home.

SYNONYM -2: **morada** *f.* • (lit.): home.

SYNONYM -3: **nido** *m.* • (lit.): nest.

chamaco/a *n.* little kid, small child.

example: Esos **chamacos** pasan todo el día jugando en el parque.

translation: Those **kids** spend all day playing at the park.

SYNONYM -1: **chiquillo/a** *n.*

NOTE: This noun comes from the adjective *chico/a* meaning "small."

SYNONYM -2: **chiquitín/a** *n.*

NOTE: This noun comes from the adjective *chico/a* meaning "small."

SYNONYM -3: **crío/a** *m.* • (lit.): a nursing-baby.

SYNONYM -4: **enano/a** *n. (Spain)* short person • (lit.): dwarf.

SYNONYM -5: **gurrumino/a** *n.* • (lit.): weak or sickly person, "whimp."

SYNONYM -6: **mocoso/a** *n.* • (lit.): snotty-nosed person.

SYNONYM -7: **párvulo** *m.* • (lit.): tot.

SYNONYM -8: **pendejo/a** *n. (Argentina).*

SYNONYM -9: **pequeñajo/a** *n.*

NOTE: This noun comes from the adjective *pequeño/a* meaning "small."

SYNONYM -10: **pituso/a** *n.* smurf (from the cartoon characters).

ANTONYM -1: **grandote** *m.*

NOTE: This noun comes from the adjective *grande* meaning "big."

ANTONYM -2: **grandullón/a** *n.* big kid.

NOTE: This noun comes from the adjective *grande* meaning "big."

chambear *v.* to work.

example: Hoy no tengo ganas de **chambear**. Estoy muy cansado.

translation: Today I don't feel like **working**. I'm really tired.

NOTE: **chamba** *f.* job.

SYNONYM -1: **currar** *v. (Spain).*

SYNONYM -2: **doblar el lomo** *exp. (Puerto Rico)* to work hard • (lit.): to fold one's back in two.

chao *interj.* good-bye.

example: ¡**Chao**! ¡Hasta la vista!

translation: **Good-bye**! See ya!

NOTE: This slang term comes from the Italian word "ciao" meaning "good-bye" and is extremely popular among Spanish speakers as well as French.

NOTE: In Argentina, this is spelled *chau.*

charlar *v.* to chat.

example: A Pepa le gusta **charlar** mucho con las amigas.

translation: Pepa loves to **chat** with her friends.

SYNONYM -1: **charlatear** *v.*

SYNONYM -2: **charlotear** *v.*

SYNONYM -3: **cuchichear** *v.*

SYNONYM -4: **parlotear** *v.*

NOTE: This term comes from the verb *parlar* meaning "to talk" or "to chat."

SYNONYM -5: **platicar** *v. (extremely common in Mexico).*

ALSO: **tener una charla** *exp.* to have a conversation.

chela *f.* beer • (lit.): blond.

example: En ese restaurante sirven **chelas** de México.

translation: They serve Mexican **beer** in that restaurant.

SYNONYM -1: **birra** *f. (Argentina).*

SYNONYM -2: **palo** *m. (Puerto Rico)* beer or any strong drink • (lit.): stick (since when one gets drunk, it could be compared to being hit on the head with a stick, causing dizziness and fogginess).

chico *m.* boy, guy, "dude."

example: Ese **chico** siempre se viste bien.

translation: That **guy** always dresses well.

NOTE: **chica** *f.* girl, "chick."

SYNONYM -1: **chamaco/a** *n. (Mexico / Puerto Rico).*

SYNONYM -2: **guambito** *m. (Columbia).*

SYNONYM -3: **nene** *m. (Argentina, Uruguay, Spain) guy* • **nena** *f.* girl.

SYNONYM -4: **patojo/a** *n. (Guatemala).*

SYNONYM -5: **pibe** *n. (Argentina, Uruguay, Spain).*

SYNONYM -6: **tío** *m. (Cuba / Spain)* • (lit.): uncle.

chismear *v.* to gossip.

example: A Pablo le encanta **chismear** sobre Anabel.

translation: Pablo loves to **gossip** about Anabel.

VARIATION: **chismorrear** *v.*

ALSO: **chisme** *m.* a juicy piece of gossip.

example: ¡Cuéntame los **chismes**!

translation: Give me the **dirt**!

SYNONYM -1: **chusmear** *v. (Argentina).*

SYNONYM -2: **cotillear** *v. (Spain).*

chocante *adj.* annoying, unpleasant.

example: Ese tío habla demasiado, es muy **chocante**.

translation: That guy talks too much. He's really **annoying**.

NOTE: **chocar** *v.* to annoy, to get annoyed, to hate something or someone • (lit.): to crash, to collide.

example: Me **choca** ir de compras cuando hay mucha gente en las tiendas.

translation: I **hate** to go shopping when there are a lot of people in the stores.

chollo *m.* good deal.

example: Solo pagué 300 dólares por este automóvil. ¡Qué **chollo**!

translation: I only paid $300 for this car. What a **deal**!

SYNONYM -1: **buena ganga (una)** *f. (Puerto Rico).*

SYNONYM -2: **curro** *m. (Argentina).*

chorra *f.* good luck.

example: ¡No te puedes imaginar la **chorra** que he tenido! ¡Me tocó la lotería!

translation: You won't believe my **luck**! I won the lottery!

ALSO: **tener chorra** *exp.* to be lucky.

chorrada *f.* stupid or despicable act.

example: No me puedo creer que Pablo hizo una **chorrada** como esa.

translation: I can't believe Pablo would do a **stupid thing** like that.

NOTE: The noun *chorrada* may also be used when referring to something very easy to do.

SYNONYM -1: **burrada** *f. (Mexico)* a stupid act or remark • (lit.): a drove of donkeys • *decir burradas;* to talk nonsense.

SYNONYM -2: **porquería** *f. (Cuba)* • (lit.): filth.

SYNONYM -3: **trastada** *f. (Puerto Rico)*. despicable act or dirty trick.

chulada *f.* said of something "cool," neat.

example: ¡Este automóvil es una verdadera **chulada**!

translation: This car is so **cool**!

SYNONYM -1: **copado/a** *adj. (Argentina)*.

SYNONYM -2: **rebueno/a** *adj. (Argentina)*.

SYNONYM -3: **tumba (estar que)** *exp. (Puerto Rico)* • (lit.): to fall (for).

ANTONYM: **chungo/a** *adj.* "uncool," ugly, lousy.

chulear *v.* to act cool, to be vain or conceited, to show off.

example: Le encanta **chulear** de coche porque tiene un coche muy caro.

translation: He loves to **show off** his car because he drives an expensive car.

NOTE: **chulo/a** *adj.* cool, neat, good looking.

example: Ese hombre es muy **chulo**, siempre se viste con ropa cara.

translation: That guy is really **cool**. He always wears expensive clothes.

SYNONYM: **echándosear** *v. (Puerto Rico / Cuba)*.

chungo/a *adj.* "uncool," lousy, ugly.

example: Esa película es muy **chunga**. Cuando fui a verla me quedé dormido.

translation: That's a really **lousy** movie. When I went to see it I fell asleep.

SYNONYM -1: **chango/a** *adj. (Puerto Rico)*.

SYNONYM -2: **flojo/a** *adj. (Mexico / Puerto Rico)*.

ANTONYM: **chulo/a** *adj.* cool, neat, great, good-looking.

chupar *v.* to drink • (lit.): to suck, to absorb.

example: A Manolo le gusta **chupar** demasiado.

translation: Manolo likes to **drink** too much.

SYNONYM -1: **darle al chupe** *exp.* to drink • (lit.): to take the pacifier (baby's comforter).

SYNONYM -2: **dar palos** *exp. (Puerto Rico)* • (lit.): to give (oneself) sticks (which is a slang synonym for "drinks" since when one gets drunk, it could be compared to being hit on the head with a stick, causing dizziness and fogginess).

chupón *m.* a player who tends to hog the ball.

example: Ernesto es un **chupón**. Nunca pasa la pelota a los demás jugadores.

translation: Ernesto **hogs the ball**. He never passes the ball to the rest of the players.

NOTE: This term is used mostly in soccer games.

SYNONYM: **peleón** *m. (Puerto Rico)* one who plays like the famous soccer player, Pele.

chusma *f.* despicable people, "scumbags."

example: Yo no voy a invitar a Jorge y Pedro a mi fiesta porque son **chusma**.

translation: I'm not inviting Jorge and Pedro to my party because they're **scum**.

cita sorpresa *exp.* blind date • (lit.): surprised date.

example: Estoy nervioso porque mañana tengo una **cita sorpresa**.

translation: I'm nervous because I have a **blind date** tomorrow.

SYNONYM -1: **cita a ciegas** *f. (Spain)* • (lit.): blind date.

SYNONYM -2: **cita amorosa** *f. (Mexico)* • (lit.): love date.

cochazo *m.* great car.

example: Alvaro tiene un **cochazo**. No sé cómo se puede permitir ese lujo.

translation: Alvaro has a **great car**. I don't know how he can afford it.

SYNONYMS: SEE - **bólido**, *p. 200.*

coco *m.* head • (lit.): coconut.

example: ¡Caramba! ¡Ese tipo tiene el **coco** enorme!

translation: Geez! That guy has a huge **head**!

SYNONYM -1: **azotea** *f. (Spain)* • (lit.): flat roof, terraced roof.

SYNONYM -2: **bocho** *m. (Argentina).*

SYNONYM -3: **cachola** *f.* • (lit.): hounds.

SYNONYM -4: **cholla** *f.* • (lit.): mind, brain.

SYNONYM -5: **coco** *m.* • (lit.): coconut.

SYNONYM -6: **cráneo** *m.* • (lit.): cranium, skull.

SYNONYM -7: **mate** *m. (Argentina).*

SYNONYM -8: **melón** *m. (Argentina).*

SYNONYM -9: **molondra** *f.*

SYNONYM -10: **sesera** *f.* • (lit.): from the masculine noun *seso* meaning "brain."

SYNONYM -11: **terraza** *f. (Argentina).*

SYNONYM -12: **testa** *f.* • (lit.): from the Latin term *testa* meaning "head."

ALSO: **tener seco el coco** *exp.* to be / to go crazy • (lit.): to have the dried coconut.

VARIATION: **secársele a uno el coco** *exp.* • (lit.): to be in the process of getting one's coconut dried.

colarse *v.* **1.** to cut in line, to slip in **2.** to gate-crash.

example: Manuel intentó **colarse** en la fiesta de Rosalía pero no pudo.

translation: Manuel tried to **sneak into** Rosalia's party but he wasn't able to.

SYNONYM -1: **deslizarse** *v.* • (lit.): to slide, to slip.

SYNONYM -2: **escurrirse** *v.* • (lit.): to drain, to drip, to trickle, to slip.

SYNONYM -3: **meterse delante de** *exp.* • (lit.): to put in front of.

colmo (ser el) *exp.* to take the cake, to be the last straw • (lit.): to be the culmination.

example: David no ha pagado el alquiler en tres meses. ¡Esto **es el colmo**!

translation: David hasn't paid the rent for three months. That **takes the cake**!

VARIATION: **colmo de los colmos (ser el)** *exp.* • (lit.): to be the culmination of culminations.

comecocos *m.* a person who tries to push his/her opinion on others.

example: Javier es un **comecocos**. Piensa que lo que le gusta a él, le debe gustar a todos.

translation: Javier always **tries to push his opinion on others**. He thinks that whatever he likes, everybody should like, too.

SYNONYM -1: **comebolas** *m.* *(Cuba)*.

SYNONYM -2: **rollo** *m.* *(Spain)* • (lit.): roll.

comerse el coco *exp.* • **1.** to worry, to get all worked up about something • **2.** to convince someone to do something • (lit.): to eat someone's head (since the masculine noun *coco*, literally meaning "coconut," is used in Spanish slang to mean "head" or "noggin").

example (1): No **te comas el coco**. Mañana será otro día.

translation: Don't **get all worked up about it**. Tomorrow will be a new beginning.

example (2): Voy a **comerle el coco** a Javier para que me dé dinero.

translation: I'm going to **convince** Javier to give me some money.

SYNONYM -1: **darse manija** *exp.* *(Argentina)* • (lit.): to give oneself a handle.

SYNONYM -2: **perder la cabeza** *exp.* *(Cuba)* • (lit.): to lose one's head.

SYNONYM -3: **rascar el coco** *exp.* *(Mexico)* • (lit.): to scratch one's head or "coconut."

como (ser) *exp.* (referring to time) approximately, about • (lit.): to be like.

example: Tengo mucho sueño. ¡Ya **son como** las dos de la madrugada!

translation: I'm very sleepy. It's **about** two o'clock in the morning!

conocer [a alguien] *exp.* • **1.** to meet (NOTE: This usage of *conocer* is extremely popular throughout the Spanish-speaking communities • **2.** to be acquainted [with someone].

example: Ayer **conocí** a mis nuevos vecinos. Parecen muy buena gente.

translation: Yesterday I **met** my new neighbors. They seem to be good people.

ALSO -1: **conocer alguien de nombre** *exp.* to know someone by name.

ALSO -2: **conocer alguien de vista** *exp.* to know someone by sight.

correr *v.* to go fast or faster, to drive fast or faster • (lit.): to run.

example: Quiero **correr** más pero no puedo porque hay mucho tráfico.

translation: I want to **go faster** but I can't because there is a lot of traffic.

SYNONYM -1: **acelerar el paso** *exp.* to speed up • (lit.): to accelerate the step.

SYNONYM -2: **apretar el acelerador** *exp.* to put the pedal to the metal • (lit.): to squeeze the accelerator.

ALSO: **carretera y manta** *exp.* *(very popular)* to hit the road • (lit.): road and blanket.

corte (dar un) *exp.* to cut someone off, to answer someone back in an aggressive way • (lit.): to cut.

example: Quise ayudar a Ismael pero me **dió un corte** y me dijo no, gracias.

translation: I wanted to help Ismael but he **cut me off** and said no thank you.

ALSO: **¡Qué corte!** *exp.* • **1.** What a disappointment! • **2.** How embarrassing!

NOTE: Interestingly enough, simply by removing the indefinite article *un* from the expression *dar un corte,* another popular expression is created: **dar corte** *exp.* to be ashamed or embarrassed.

SYNONYM -1: **cortarón (dar un)** *exp. (Argentina).*

SYNONYM -2: **corte pastelillo (dar un)** *exp. (Puerto Rico).*

NOTE: **pastelillo** *m.* • (lit.): a fried pastry that has been folded in half and cut.

creído/a *adj.* snob, conceited person • (lit.): thought or believed.

example: Manuel es un **creído**. Se cree que es mejor que nadie.

translation: Manuel is a **snob**. He thinks he's better than anybody else.

SYNONYM -1: **esnob** *m.*

SYNONYM -2: **snob** *m.*

SYNONYM -3: **zarpado/a** *n.* *(Argentina).*

cruda *f.* hangover • (lit.): raw.

example: Si bebes mucho hoy, mañana tendrás una **cruda**.

translation: If you drink a lot today, you'll have a **hangover** tomorrow.

SYNONYM -1: **goma (estar de)** *exp.* to be like rubber.

SYNONYM -2: **resaca** *f.* • (lit.): undertow.

cuadrado/a (estar) *adj.* (pronounced *cuadrao* in Cuba and Puerto Rico) to be strong, muscular • (lit.): to be squared.

example: Ricardo está **cuadrado**, se nota que hace ejercicio.

translation: Ricardo is so **strong**, you can tell he exercises.

SYNONYM: **mula (estar como una)** *exp.* • (lit.): to be like a mule.

cuate *m. (Mexico)* buddy, friend • (lit.): twin.

example: Alfredo es mi **cuate**. Siempre puedo contar con él.

translation: Alfredo is my **buddy**. I can always count on him.

SYNONYM -1: **amigote** *m.* • (lit.): big friend (from the noun *amigo*).

SYNONYM -2: **camarada** *m.* • (lit.): comrade.

SYNONYM -3: **carnal** *m.* • (lit.): related by blood.

SYNONYM -4: **compadre** *m.* • (lit.): godfather.

SYNONYM -5: **hermano** *m.* • (lit.): brother.

SYNONYM -6: **jefe** *m.* • (lit.): boss.

SYNONYM -7: **mano** *m.*

NOTE: This is a shortened version of *hermano* meaning "brother."

SYNONYM -8: **tío** *m. (Cuba / Spain)* • (lit.): uncle.

cuatroojos *m.* a person who wears glasses, "four-eyes" • (lit.): four eyes.

example: Mi maestro de literatura es un **cuatroojos**.

translation: My literature teacher is **four-eyed**.

NOTE: Also spelled: *cuatrojos*.

SYNONYM -1: **bisco/a** *n. (Argentina).*

SYNONYM -2: **cegato/a** *adj.* • (lit.): from the masculine noun *ciego* meaning "blind person."

SYNONYM -3: **chicato/a** *adj. (Argentina).*

SYNONYM -4: **corto de vista** *exp.* nearsighted • (lit.): shortsighted.

SYNONYM -5: **gafitas** *adj.* • (lit.): from the masculine noun *gafas* meaning "glasses."

SYNONYM -6: **gafudo/a** *adj.* • (lit.): from the masculine noun *gafas* meaning "glasses."

cuentista *m. & f.* gossip • (lit.): story teller.

example: Sergio siempre está hablando de otras personas. ¡Es un **cuentista**!

translation: Sergio is always talking about other people. He's such a **gossip**!

SYNONYM -1: **cantamañanas** *m.*

SYNONYM -2: **chismoso** *m. (Argentina).*

SYNONYM -3: **mitotero/a** *n. (Mexico).*

cuentón *m.* • **1.** big bill, check • **2.** long story.

example (1): ¡Casi me da un ataque cardíaco cuando me llegó el **cuentón** y me di cuenta cuanto costaba comer en ese restaurante!

translation: I almost had a heart attack when I got the **check** and found out how much our meal cost at the restaurant!

example (2): Si quieres, te cuento lo que me pasó hoy en la escuela pero es un **cuentón**.

translation: If you want, I'll tell you what happened to me at school today but it's a **long story**.

SYNONYM -1: **dolorosa** *f. (Puerto Rico)* • (lit.): that which causes pain (from the masculine noun *dolor* meaning "pain").

SYNONYM -2: **importe** *m.*

SYNONYM -3: **monto** *m.*

NOTE: The synonyms above apply to definition **1** only.

ANTONYM: **cuentecilla** *f.* small bill or check.

currar *v.* to work.

example: Me encanta **currar** en este restaurante porque así nunca tengo hambre.

translation: I love **working** at this restaurant because that way I never go hungry.

SYNONYM -1: **afanar** *v. (Argentina).*

SYNONYM -2: **chambear** *v.*

NOTE: **chamba** *m.* job.

darse lija *exp.* to put on airs, to act pretentious, to have an attitude problem • (lit.): to give oneself sandpaper.

example: A Ricardo le gusta **darse lija**. Cree que es mejor que nadie.

translation: Ricardo likes to **put on airs**. He thinks he's better than anybody else.

SYNONYM: **ser un broncas** *adj. (Spain)* to have a bad attitude, said of someone who is always in fights.

de gala (estar) *exp.* to be all dress up, to be dressed to kill • (lit.): to be in full regalia.

example: Siempre que voy a una fiesta me visto **de gala**.

translation: I always get **all dressed up** when I go to a party.

VARIATION: **vestirse de gala** *exp.* to get all dressed up.

deshacerse de alguien *exp.* to get rid of someone • (lit.): to undo oneself of someone.

example: Juan es tan aburrido. Quería **deshacerme de** él pero no sabía cómo.

translation: Juan is so boring. I wanted to get **rid of** him, but I didn't know how.

SYNONYM: **dar un esquinazo a alguien** *exp.* • (lit.): to give a corner to someone.

ALSO: **deshacerse por uno** *exp.* to go out of one's way for someone, to outdo oneself for someone, to bend over backward for someone • (lit.): to undo oneself for.

desmadre *m.* chaotic mess.

example: ¡Esta boda es un **desmadre**! Nadie sabe donde sentarse.

translation: This wedding is a **chaotic mess**! Nobody knows where to sit.

ALSO -1: **¡Qué desmadre!** *interj.* What a mess!

ALSO -2: **armar un desmadre** *exp.* to kick up a rumpus.

SYNONYMS: SEE - **gazpacho**, *p. 215.*

dominguero *m.* a bad driver, Sunday driver.

example: Parece que todos los **domingueros** decidieron salir al mismo tiempo.

translation: It looks like all the **Sunday drivers** decided to go out at the same time.

NOTE: This comes from the noun *domingo* meaning "Sunday."

SYNONYM: **bago** *m. (Mexico).*

donnadie *m.* loser • (lit.): Mr. Nobody.

example: Es tipo es un **donnadie**, no tiene dinero ni para pagar el alquiler.

translation: That guy is such a **loser**. He doesn't even have enough money to pay rent.

SYNONYM: **matada/o** *n. (Spain).*

ANTONYM: **casinadie** *m.* a very important person • (lit.): almost nobody - SEE: *p. 203.*

dulzura *f.* sweetheart.

example: Lynda es una **dulzura**. Siempre está sonriendo.

translation: Lynda is a **sweetheart**. She's always smiling.

SYNONYM -1: **amor** *m.* • (lit.): love.

SYNONYM -2: **bombón** *m.* • (lit.): a type of chocolate candy.

SYNONYM -3: **caramelo** *m.* • (lit.): candy.

SYNONYM -4: **ternura** *f.* • (lit.): tenderness.

empollón/na *n.* nerd, geek, pain in the neck.

example: Francisco siempre está estudiando. Es un verdadero **empollón**.

translation: Francisco is always studying. He's a real **nerd**.

NOTE: **empollar** *v.* to study hard • (lit.): to hatch, brood.

SYNONYMS: SEE - **adoquín**, *p. 195.*

enano/a *n.* short person • (lit.): dwarf.

example: Mi maestro de literatura es tan **enano** que ni siquiera alcanza el pizarrón.

translation: My literature teacher is so **short** he can't even reach the blackboard.

SYNONYM: **hombrecito** *m. (Cuba).*

enchufe *m.* cushy job • (lit.): plug, socket.

example: Manuel consiguió un buen trabajo porque tiene un buen **enchufe**.

translation: Manuel got a **cushy job** because he has good connections.

ALSO: **tener enchufe** *exp.* to have connections.

SYNONYM -1: **chollo** *m.*

SYNONYM -2: **laburo** *m. (Argentina).*

SYNONYM -3: **momio** *m.*
• (lit.): that which is lean.

SYNONYM -4: **pala** *f. (Puerto Rico)*
• (lit.): shovel.

enrollarse *v.* **1.** to talk up a storm • **2.** to get involved romantically with someone • (lit.): to roll up, to wind.

example (1): A mi madre le gusta **enrollarse** mucho cuando viene visita a la casa.

translation: My mother loves to **talk up a storm** when she has company at her house.

example (2): Me encantaría **enrollarme** a esa tía porque es muy simpática y guapa.

translation: I'd love to **get involved** with that girl because she's very nice and beautiful.

SYNONYM: **cotorrear** *v. (Puerto Rico / Cuba)* • (lit.): to squawk (like a parrot).

NOTE: **charlatán/ana** *n.* blabbermouth.

enterarse *v.* to find out • (lit.): to inform oneself.

example: ¿**Te enteraste** de cómo se llega a la casa de Alfredo?

translation: Did you **find out** how got to Alfredo's house?

escuincle *m.* little kid, small child.

example: ¡No me lo puedo creer! Luisa ya tiene siete **escuincles** y ¡está embarazada otra vez!

translation: I can't believe it! Luisa already has seven **kids** and she's pregnant again!

SYNONYM -1: **chiquillo/a** *n.*

NOTE: This noun comes from the adjective *chico/a* meaning "small."

SYNONYM -2: **chiquitín/a** *n.*

NOTE: This noun comes from the adjective *chico/a* meaning "small."

SYNONYM -3: **crío/a** *m. (Spain)*
• (lit.): a nursing-baby.

SYNONYM -4: **gurrumino/a** *n.*
• (lit.): weak or sickly person, "whimp."

SYNONYM -5: **mocoso/a** *n.*
• (lit.): snotty-nosed person.

SYNONYM -6: **nené** *m. (Puerto Rico / Cuba).*

NOTE: By putting an accent over the second "e" in *nene*, this standard term for "baby" acquires a slang connotation.

SYNONYM -7: **párvulo** *m.*
• (lit.): tot.

SYNONYM -8: **pequeñajo/a** *n.*

NOTE: This noun comes from the adjective *pequeño/a* meaning "small."

SYNONYM -9: **pituso/a** *n.* smurf (from the cartoon characters).

ANTONYM -1: **grandote** *m.*

NOTE: This noun comes from the adjective *grande* meaning "big."

ANTONYM -2: **grandullón/a** *n.* big kid.

NOTE: This noun comes from the adjective *grande* meaning "big."

evaporarse *v.* to disappear, to vanish • (lit.): to evaporate.

example: Me **evaporé** cuando me di cuenta que Juan estaba en la fiesta.

translation: I **disappeared** when I realized Juan was at the party.

SYNONYM -1: **colarse** *v. (Mexico)* • (lit.): to filter oneself.

SYNONYM -2: **escaquearse** *v. (Spain)* • (lit.): to check or checker oneself.

SYNONYM -3: **escurrirse** *v.* • (lit.): to slip, to slide, to sneak out.

SYNONYM -4: **esfumarse** *v.* • (lit.): to vanish.

fichado/a (estar) *adj.* to be on someone's bad side, to be on someone's bad list • (lit.): to be posted or affixed.

example: Creo que el maestro tiene **fichado** a Pepe porque siempre le está gritando.

translation: I think Pepe's on the teacher's **bad side** because he's always yelling at him.

VARIATION: **fichado/a (tener)** *exp.* • (lit.): to have posted or affixed.

SYNONYM -1: **cazar alguien** *v. (Cuba)* • (lit.): to hunt someone down.

SYNONYM -2: **tener en la mirilla** *exp.* • (lit.): to have someone on target.

flote (estar a) *exp.* to be well off (monetarily).

example: Parece que Pedro está **a flote**. ¿Viste qué cochazo tiene?

translation: It seems like Pedro is **well off**. Did you see what a great car he drives?

SEE: **lana**, *p. 217*.

foca *f.* a very fat woman • (lit.): seal.

example: Adriana es una **foca**. Parece que siempre está comiendo.

translation: Adriana is really **fat**. It seems like she's always eating.

SYNONYM -1: **elefante** *m.* • (lit.): elephant.

SYNONYM -2: **gordita** *f. (Cuba)*.

SYNONYM -3: **vaca** *f. (Puerto Rico* • (lit.): cow.

follón *m.* • **1.** mess, jam • **2.** trouble, uproar.

example (1): El tráfico de Chicago es un **follón**.

translation: The traffic in Chicago is a **mess**.

example (2): Si nuestro equipo pierde el partido se va a armar un gran **follón**.

translation: If our team loses the games, there is going to be an **uproar** here.

SYNONYMS: SEE - **gazpacho**, *p. 215*.

ALSO -1: **armar un follón** *exp.* to kick up a rumpus.

ALSO -2: **¡Menudo follón!** *exp.* What a mess!

ALSO -3: **¡Qué follón!** *exp.* What a mess!

gafudo/a • **1.** *adj.* said of one who wears glasses, "four-eyed" • **2.** *n.* one who wears glasses, "four-eyes."

example (1): El policía **gafudo** me dio una multa.

translation: That **four-eyed** policeman gave me a ticket.

example (2): Ese **gafudo** es mi nuevo profesor de biología.

translation: That **four-eyed man** is my new biology teacher.

SYNONYM -1: **anteojudo** *m.* *(Argentina).*

SYNONYM -2: **cuatroojos** *m.* • (lit.): four-eyes.

SYNONYM -3: **gafas** *f.pl. (Cuba)* • (lit.): glasses.

SYNONYM -4: **gafitas** *adj. & n.* • (lit.): small pair of glasses.

galán *adj.* hunk, good-looking guy.

example: Claudio es un **galán**. Se nota que se cuida.

translation: Claudio is a **hunk**. You can tell he takes care of himself.

SYNONYM -1: **chorbo** *adj. (Spain).*

SYNONYM -2: **gallardo** *adj.* • (lit.): elegant, graceful.

NOTE: There is no feminine form of this adjective since it can only refer to a man.

SYNONYM -3: **majo** *adj.* • (lit.): showy, flashy, dressed up.

SYNONYM -4: **tío bueno** *m.* *(Spain).*

gazpacho *m. (Spain)* mess, predicament, jam • (lit.): a type of Spanish tomato soup.

example: El tráfico de Los Angeles es un verdadero **gazpacho**.

translation: Los Angeles traffic is a real **mess**.

SYNONYM -1: **broncón** *m.* *(Mexico).*

SYNONYM -2: **caos** *m.* • (lit.): chaos.

SYNONYM -3: **desbarajuste** *m.* • (lit.): disorder, confusion.

SYNONYM -4: **despelote** *m.*

SYNONYM -5: **embole** *m.* *(Argentina).*

SYNONYM -6: **embrollo** *m.* • (lit.): muddle, tangle, confusion.

SYNONYM -7: **enredo** *m.* • (lit.): tangle, snarl (in wool).

SYNONYM -8: **follón** *m.* • (lit.): lazy, idle.

SYNONYM -9: **garrón** *m.* *(Argentina).*

SYNONYM -10: **golpaso** *m.* *(Mexico)* • (lit.): heavy or violent blow.

SYNONYM -11: **jaleo** *m.* • (lit.): noisy party.

SYNONYM -12: **kilombo** *m.* *(Argentina).*

SYNONYM -13: **lío** *m.* • (lit.): bundle, package.

SYNONYM -14: **marrón** *m. (Spain).*

SYNONYM -15: **mogollón** *m.*

SYNONYM -16: **paquete** *m.* *(Cuba)* • (lit.): package.

SYNONYM -17: **revoltijo** *m.* • (lit.): jumble, mix-up.

SYNONYM -18: **revoltillo** *m.* • (lit.): jumble, mix-up.

SYNONYM -19: **revuelo** *m.* *(Cuba)* • (lit.): second flight.

ALSO: **revoltillo de huevos** *m.* scrambled eggs • (lit.): a jumble of eggs.

SYNONYM -20: **sángano** *m.* *(Puerto Rico)*.

gentío *m.* crowd, people.

example: No me gusta ir a los partidos de béisbol porque siempre hay mucho **gentío**.

translation: I don't like going to baseball games because there are always big **crowds** there.

SYNONYM: **gente** *f.* people, folks, relatives.

ALSO: **gente gorda** *f.* bigwigs • (lit.): fat people.

gordinflón *adj.* fat pig, obese person.

example: Darío es un **gordinflón**. Parece que nunca para de comer.

translation: Darío is a **fat pig**. It seems like he never stops eating.

SYNONYM -1: **mofletudo/a** *adj.* • (lit.): chubby-cheeked.

SYNONYM -2: **rechoncho/a** *adj.* • (lit.): chubby, tubby.

SYNONYM -3: **regordete** *adj.*

NOTE: This comes from the adjective *gordo/a* meaning "fat."

SYNONYM -4: **tripón** *adj.*

NOTE: This comes from the feminine noun *tripa* meaning "tripe," "guts" or "stomach."

ANTONYM: **canijo** *adj.* skinny person.

gozador/a *adj.* big spender, person who likes to have fun all the time.

example: Francisco es un gran **gozador**. Le encanta pasarlo bien.

translation: Francisco is such a **big spender**. He loves to have fun.

NOTE: This comes from the verb *gozar* meaning "to enjoy."

SYNONYM -1: **gastador** *m.* *(Argentina / Cuba)*.

SYNONYM -2: **maniroto** *m.* *(Spain)*.

guay *adj.* cool, neat.

example: ¡Qué **guay**! ¡Esa motocicleta tiene tres ruedas!

translation: **Cool**! That motorcycle has three wheels!

SYNONYM -1: **chulo** *adj.*

SYNONYM -2: **padre** *adj.* • (lit.): father.

hombre • **1.** *m.* husband • **2.** *interj.* wow! • (lit.): man.

example (1): No me puedo quejar. Mi **hombre** me trata muy bien.

translation: I can't complain. My **husband** treats me very well.

example (2): ¡**Hombre**! ¡Esta mujer es guapísima!

translation: **Wow**! That girl is beautiful!

SYNONYM -1: **¡Ay Caray!** *interj.* *(Cuba).*

SYNONYM -2: **¡Caballero!** *interj.* • (lit.): Sir!

SYNONYM -3: **¡Che!** *interj.* *(Argentina).*

SYNONYM -4: **¡Guau!** *interj.* *(Spain / Puerto Rico* - pronounced *Wow!).*

VARIATION: **¡Guao!**

SYNONYM -5: **¡Manitas!** *interj.* *(Puerto Rico).*

SYNONYM -6: **¡Mujer!** *interj.* *(Cuba)* • (lit.): woman.

SYNONYM -7: **¡Tío!** *interj.* • (lit.): Uncle!

SYNONYM -8: **¡Ufa!** *interj.* *(Argentina).*

horripilante *adj.* horrifying, terrifying.

example: Esa película es **horripilante**. Me tuve que salir del cine.

translation: That's a **horrifying** movie. I had to get out of the theater.

SYNONYM -1: **espeluznante** *adj.* • (lit.): horrifying.

SYNONYM -2: **horroroso** *adj.* • (lit.): horrible, dreadful, hideous.

SYNONYM -3: **pavorosa** *adj.* • (lit.): frightful, terrifying.

huevón *adj.* lazy.

example: Mario es un **huevón**. Nunca hace nada.

translation: Mario is a **lazy bum**. He never does anything.

SYNONYM -1: **dejado/a** *adj.* • (lit.): left (from the verb *dejar* meaning "to leave [something].")

SYNONYM -2: **flojo/a** *adj. & n.* • (lit.): lazy, idle.

SYNONYM -3: **parado/a** *adj.* *(Spain).*

NOTE: This is pronounced: *parao / parah* in Spain.

SYNONYM -4: **vago/a** *adj.* *(Spain)* • (lit.): vague.

ALSO: **hacer la hueva** *exp.* not to lift a finger, to do nothing • (lit.): to make a female egg.

jeta *f.* face.

example: ¡Qué **jeta**! ¡Marisa es guapísima!

translation: What a **face**! Marisa is beautiful!

ALSO: ¡Qué **jeta**! *exp.* What nerve!

lana *f.* *(Spain)* money • (lit.): wool.

example: Se nota que Javier tiene **lana**. Siempre conduce un automóvil último modelo.

translation: You can tell Javier has **money**. He always drives a late-model car.

SYNONYM -1: **guita** *f. (Argentina)* • (lit.): twine.

SYNONYM -2: **pasta** *f.* • (lit.): pasta, paste.

SYNONYM -3: **plata** *f.* • (lit.): silver.

SYNONYM -4: **tela** *f. (Argentina)* • (lit.): material, cloth, fabric.

largarse *v.* to leave, to go away, to beat it.

example: Como no me gustó el concierto, me **largué** en seguida.

translation: Since I didn't like the concert, I **left** after only a little while.

SYNONYM -1: **escabullirse** *v.* • (lit.): to slip (from, through, or out), to escape.

SYNONYM -2: **escurrirse** *v.* • (lit.): to drain, to slide.

SYNONYM -3: **evaporarse** *v.* • (lit.): to evaporate oneself.

SYNONYM -4: **marcharse** *v.* • (lit.): to go away, to leave.

lata *f.* • **1.** pain in the neck, annoyance, nuisance • **2.** boring person or thing • **3.** long boring speech or conversation • (lit.): tin can.

example: Esta película es una verdadera **lata**.

translation: This movie is so **boring**.

SYNONYM -1: **garrón** *m. (Argentina).*

SYNONYM -2: **moserga** *f.* • (lit.): bore, nuisance.

SYNONYM -3: **rollo** *m.* • (lit.): roll • SEE - *p. 228.*

SYNONYM -4: **tabarra** *f.* • (lit.): bore, nuisance.

ALSO -1: **dar la lata** *exp.* • **1.** to annoy • **2.** to bore • (lit.): to give the can.

ALSO -2: **¡Qué lata!** *interj.* What a pain in the butt! • (lit.): What a tin can!

latón *n.* annoying person, pain in the neck.

example: Por favor, no invites a Maria a la fiesta mañana. ¡Es un **latón**!

translation: Please don't invite Maris to the party tonight. She's such a **pain in the neck**!

SYNONYM -1: **chinche** *m. (Puerto Rico / Cuba)* • (lit.): an annoying little bug.

SYNONYM -2: **dolor de cabeza (ser un)** *exp. (Cuba)* • (lit.): to be a pain in the head or headache.

SYNONYM -3: **lata** *f.* a pain in the neck • (lit.): tin can.

NOTE: Both *latón* and *lata* may be used when referring either to people or to things: *¡Qué lata!* or *¡Qué latón!* = What a pain in the neck!

SYNONYM -4: **latoso/a** *n. (Mexico).*

SYNONYM -5: **marrón** *m. (Spain).*

leñazo *m.* blow, bump, accident • (lit.): large piece of firewood.

example: Ayer Luis se dió un **leñazo** en el coche.

translation: Yesterday Luis had a car **accident**.

SYNONYM -1: **batacazo** *m.* • (lit.): thud.

SYNONYM -2: **golpetazo** *m.* • (lit.): great blow or knock.

VARIATION: **golpazo** *m.*

NOTE: From the verb *golpear* meaning "to hit."

SYNONYM -3: **porrazo** *m.*
• (lit.): great blow or knock.

SYNONYM -4: **topetazo** *m.*
• (lit.): great blow or knock.

SYNONYM -5: **trancazo** *m.*
• (lit.): great blow or knock.

SYNONYM -6: **trompazo** *m.*
• (lit.): great blow or knock.

ALSO: **dar/pegar un leñazo** *exp.* to hit something or someone, to have an accident.

liarse *v.* to get involved (with someone), to go out with • (lit.): to tie up, to wrap up.

example: Parece que Alfonso se ha **liado** con Lynda.

translation: It seems like Alfonso is **involved** with Lynda.

SYNONYM -1: **engancharse** *v.* *(Argentina)* • (lit.): to get hooked up (with someone).

SYNONYM -2: **enrollarse** *v.*
• (lit.): to roll up.

SYNONYM -3: **juntarse** *v.*
• (lit.): to join, to unite.

SYNONYM -4: **ligarse** *v.* *(Cuba / Mexico)* • (lit.): to tie oneself up (with someone).

ALSO: **liarse a golpes** *exp.* to come to blows.

listillo/a *adj.* *(Spain)* smart, clever person.

example: David es un **listillo**. Siempre tiene la respuesta adecuada.

translation: David is so **smart**. He always has the right answer.

SYNONYM -1: **agosado/a** *adj.* *(Puerto Rico / Cuban).*

NOTE: In Puerto Rico and Cuba, this is pronounced: *agosao / agosah.*

SYNONYM -2: **avispado/a** *adj.*
• (lit.): clever, sharp.

NOTE: This comes from the term *avispa* meaning "wasp."

SYNONYM -3: **despabilado/a** *adj.* • (lit.): awakened.

NOTE: This comes from the verb *despavilar* meaning "to wake up."

SYNONYM -4: **pillo** *adj.*
• (lit.): roguish, mischievous.

SYNONYM -5: **vivo/a** *adj.*
• (lit.): alive.

ANTONYM -1: **adoquín** *m.* jerk, fool, moron, simpleton
• (lit.): paving block.

ANTONYM -2: **bruto/a** *adj.*
• (lit.): stupid, crude.

ANTONYM -3: **cabezota** *adj.*

NOTE: This comes from the feminine noun *cabeza* meaning "head." The suffix *-ota* is commonly used to modify the meaning of the noun changing it literally to "big head."

ANTONYM -4: **tosco/a** *adj.*
• (lit.): coarse, crude, unrefined.

ANTONYM -5: **zopenco/a** *adj.*
• (lit.): dull, stupid.

malísimamente *adv.* really badly, terribly (from the adverb *mal* meaning "poorly").

example: Juan jugó **malísimamente**.

translation: Juan played **really badly**.

SYNONYM -1: **de pena** *exp.* • (lit.): of shame.

SYNONYM -2: **pésimamente** *adv.* • (lit.): very badly, wretchedly.

ANTONYM: **buenísimamente** *adv.* (from the adverb *bueno* meaning "good") fantastically.

mangante *m.* thief.

example: Anoche entró un **mangante** a mi casa y se llevó mis joyas.

translation: Last night a **thief** broke into my house and stole my jewelry.

SYNONYM -1: **caco** *m.* • (lit.): thief.

SYNONYM -2: **chorizo** *m.* • (lit.): a type of Spanish sausage.

SYNONYM -3: **chorro** *m.* *(Argentina)*.

SYNONYM -4: **pillo** *m.* *(Puerto Rico)*.

SYNONYM -5: **ratero** *m.* *(Mexico)* • (lit.): petty thief.

mangar *v.* to steal, to rob.

example: Ese tipo quiso **robar** el banco pero lo atrapó la policía.

translation: That guy tried to **rob** the bank but he was caught by the police.

SYNONYM -1: **afanar** *v.* *(Argentina)* • **1.** to steal, to swipe • **2.** to work hard (as seen earlier).

SYNONYM -2: **escamotear** *v.*

SYNONYM -3: **hurtar** *v.*

manitas *m.* handyman • (lit.): little hands.

example: Pepe arregla todo en su casa. ¡Es un verdadero **manitas**!

translation: Pepe fixes everything in his house himself. He's a real **handyman**!

SYNONYM: **arreglatodo** *m.* (said of a man or woman) • (lit.): a fix-everything.

ANTONYM -1: **chambón** *adj.* • (lit.): awkward.

ANTONYM -2: **desmañado/a** *adj.* • (lit.): clumsy or awkward person.

ANTONYM -3: **incapaz** *adj.* • (lit.): incapable, unable.

ANTONYM -4: **patoso/a** *adj.* • (lit.): boring, dull.

ANTONYM -5: **torpe** *adj.* clumsy

ANTONYM -6: **zopenco/a** *adj.*

matasanos *m.* doctor • (lit.): killer of healthy people (from the verb *matar* meaning "to kill" and *sano* meaning "heath").

example: El marido de Gloria es un **matasanos**.

translation: Gloria's husband is a **doctor**.

NOTE: Although this term literally has a negative meaning, it is commonly used in jest to refer to a doctor in general.

SYNONYM: **doc** *m.* *(Argentina)*.

media naranja *exp.* better half, spouse • (lit.): **1.** half an orange • **2.** dome, cupola.

example: A mi **media naranja** y a mí nos encanta ir a México de vacaciones.

translation: My **wife** and I love going to Mexico on vacation.

NOTE -1: In Spanish, a dome is called a *media naranja* (literally, "half an orange") due to its shape.

NOTE -2: *Media naranja* is commonly used as a humorous and affectionate term for one's spouse, since one half completes the other as would two halves of an orange.

SYNONYM: **jermu** *f. Argentina)* a reverse transformation of the word *mujer* (jer-mu) meaning woman or wife.

menearse *v.* to move, dance.

example: Me encanta cómo **se menea** Alberto. Baila muy bien.

translation: I love how Alberto **moves**. He really dances well.

SYNONYM -1: **bailotear** *v.*

NOTE: This term comes from the verb *bailar* meaning "to dance."

SYNONYM -2: **moverse** *v.* • (lit.): to move.

ALSO: **mover la colita** *exp.* • (lit.): to move or shake one's tail.

NOTE: This expression comes from a popular Spanish song meaning "to shake one's booty."

merengue *m.* beautiful woman, "knockout" • (lit.): meringue, a type of pie.

example: Ana es la chica más guapa de la escuela. ¡Es un verdadero **merengue**!

translation: Ana is the most beautiful girl at school. She's a real **babe**!

SYNONYM -1: **bollito** *m. (Spain)* • (lit.): a small sweet cake.

SYNONYM -2: **bombón** *m.* bonbon • (lit.): (a type of chocolate candy).

SYNONYM -3: **buena moza** *f.* • (lit.): good maid.

SYNONYM -4: **buenona** *f.*

NOTE: This noun comes from the adjective *bueno/a* meaning "good."

SYNONYM -5: **diosa** *f. (Argentina)* godess.

SYNONYM -6: **maja** *f.* • (lit.): flashy or showy.

SYNONYM -7: **mamasíta** *f.* • (lit.): little mother.

SYNONYM -8: **pimpollo** *m.* • (lit.): flower bud or bloom.

SYNONYM -9: **tía buena** *f. (Spain / Cuba)* • (lit.): good aunt.

SYNONYM -10: **venus** *f.* • (lit.): Venus (the goddess of beauty).

meter un gol *exp.* to score a goal • (lit.): to put in a goal.

example: No me puedo creer que Luis **metió seis goles** en el partido de ayer.

translation: I can't believe Luis **scored six goals** in yesterday's game.

NOTE: This expression is used primarily in soccer games although it may also be used in similar sports such as hockey, waterpolo, etc.

montón *m.* a bunch of, a lot of
• (lit.): crowd.

example: Alfonso tiene un **montón** de amigos en todas partes porque es muy simpático.

translation: Alfonso has **a lot of** friends everywhere because he's very nice.

NOTE -1: **a montones** *exp.* in large quantities, abundantly • *libros a montones;* a large quantity of books (literally, "a mountain of books").

NOTE -2: **ser del montón** *exp.* to be mediocre • (lit.): to be of the crowd.

SYNONYM: **pila** *f.* • (lit.): a pile – see *p. 225*

morrocotudo/a *adj.* • **1.** neat, cool, terrific, fabulous • **2.** very important • **3.** difficult • **4.** wealthy • **5.** big, enormous.

example (1): El nuevo automóvil de Carlos es muy **morrocotudo**.

translation: Carlos' new car is really **cool**.

example (2): Mi entrevista con el presidente es **morrocotuda**.

translation: My interview with the President is **very important**.

example (3): Este problema de matemáticas es **morrocotudo**.

translation: This math problem is very **difficult**.

example (4): Pablo es un **morrocotudo**. ¡Debes de ver la casa nueva que se ha comprado!

translation: Pablo is very **wealthy**. You should see the new house he bought!

example (5): ¡Ese barco es **morrocotudo**!

translation: That ship is **enormous**!

NOTE: The following are synonyms for example (1) only:

SYNONYM -1: **alucinante** *adj. (Argentina).*

SYNONYM -2: **chulo/a** *adj. (Spain)* neat, cool, terrific.

SYNONYM -3: **del carah** *adj. (Puerto Rico).*

SYNONYM -4: **molón** *adj. (Spain).*

ANTONYM: **chungo/a** *adj.* ugly, "uncool."

NOTE: This is an antonym for the previous example (1) only.

mugre *f.* filth, grime, dirt.

example: ¡Oye Paco! Tu automóvil está lleno de **mugre**. ¡Parece que nunca lo lavas!

translation: Hey Paco! Your car is so full of **dirt**. It looks like you never wash it!

SYNONYM -1: **cochambre** *f.* • (lit.): greasy.

SYNONYM -2: **porquería** *f.* • (lit.): junk.

narizón *adj.* big-nosed.

example: ¡Mira su **narizón**!

translation: Look at his **big nose**!

NOTE -1: This comes from the feminine noun *nariz* meaning "nose." In Spanish, special suffixes are commonly attached to nouns, adjectives, and adverbs to intensify their meaning. In this case, the suffix *zón* is added to the word *nariz*, transforming it to *narizón*, or "honker," "schnozzola," etc. To say "Look at his big nose!" in Spanish, it would certainly be more colloquial to say *¡Mira su **narizón**!* rather than *¡Mira su gran nariz!* The same would apply to other nouns as well, such as *cabeza*, meaning "head": *¡Mira su **cabezón**!* rather than *!Mira su gran cabeza!*

NOTE -2: When a noun is modified using the suffix *zón*, it may be used interchangeably as an adjective:

NOUN:

*¡Mira su **nariz**!*
(Look at his nose!)

¡Mira su ***cabeza***!
(Look at his head!)

MODIFIED NOUN:

¡Mira su ***narizón***!
(Look at his big honker!)

¡Mira su **cabezón**!
(Look at his big head!)

MODIFIED ADJECTIVE:

¡Es un tipo ***narizón***!
(He's a big-nosed guy!)

¡Es un tipo ***cabezón***!
(He's a big-headed guy!)

VARIATION: **narigón** *adj.*

ANTONYM: **chato/a** *adj.* flat-nosed, pug-nosed.

nena *f.* girl, young woman.

example: Creo que conozco a esa **nena**. La vi en en el centro comercial.

translation: I think I know that **girl**. I saw her at the mall.

SYNONYM -1: **mina** *f. (Argentina)* • (lit.): mine (as in "gold mine").

SYNONYM -2: **muchachita** *f. (Cuba)*.

SYNONYM -3: **tía** *f. (Spain / Cuba)* • (lit.): aunt.

ANTONYM: **nene** *m.* boy, young man.

nido *m.* home, house, place • (lit.): nest.

example: !Oye María! ¿Por qué no vamos a mi **nido** a ver la televisión?

translation: Hey, Maria! Why don't we go to my **place** to watch TV?

ALSO: **haberse caído de un nido** *exp.* to be very gullible • (lit.): to have just fallen from the nest.

SYNONYM -1: **bulin** *m. (Argentina)*.

SYNONYM -2: **castillo** *m.* • (lit.): castle.

SYNONYM -3: **cobijo** *m.* • (lit.): shelter.

SYNONYM -4: **morada** *f.* • (lit.): home.

SYNONYM -5: **palacio** *m.* • (lit.): palace.

SYNONYM -6: **techo** *m.* • (lit.): roof.

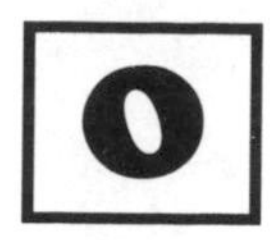

¡Olé! *interj. (Spain)* Yippee! Alright!

example: **¡Olé!** Vaya gol que ha metido Alvaro.

translation: **Yippee!** What a goal Alvaro just scored!

NOTE: This expression has its roots in the bullfights. It is still the traditional cheer from the audience when a bullfighter makes a good pass.

ALSO: **¡Y olé!** *interj. (Spain).*

SYNONYM: **¡Caramba!** *interj. (Mexico).*

pachanga *f.* party.

example: Esta **pachanga** es muy divertida. Todo el mundo se lo está pasando muy bien.

translation: This **party** is a lot of fun. Everybody is having a good time.

NOTE: **ir de pachanga** *exp.* to go out and have a good time.

SYNONYM -1: **boliche** *f. (Argentina).*

SYNONYM -2: **fiestón** *m. (Puerto Rico)*

SYNONYM -3: **movida** *f. (Spain).*

SYNONYM -4: **parranda** *f.*

SYNONYM -5: **reventón** *m.* • (lit.): bursting, explosion.

pagar al contado *exp.* to pay cash on the barrel • (lit.): to pay counted.

example: Cuando como en un restaurante, siempre intento **pagar al contado** en lugar de con tarjeta de crédito.

translation: When I eat at a restaurant, I always try to **pay cash** instead of using my credit card.

SYNONYM -1: **pagar a tocateja** *exp.* • (lit.): to pay to the touch.

SYNONYM -2: **pagar con billetes** *exp.* • (lit.): to pay with bills.

pasta *f.* money, "dough" • (lit.): pasta.

example: Se nota que Javier tiene **pasta**. Mira su coche.

translation: You can tell Javier is loaded with **money**. Look at his house.

SYNONYMS: SEE - **lana**, *p. 217.*

pavor (tener) *exp.* to be scared.

example: Sara **tenía pavor** de ir a la escuela el primer día.

translation: Sara was **scared** to go to school on the first day.

SYNONYM: **temblando (estar)** *adj.* • (lit.): to be trembling.

ALSO: **temblar de miedo** *exp.* • (lit.): to shake with fear.

pedazo de *adj.* great (when used before a noun) • (lit.): piece.

example: Alberto se acaba de comprar un **pedazo** de coche.

translation: Alberto just bought a **great** car.

ALSO: **pedazo de pan (ser un)** *exp.* to be very kind or easy-going • (lit.): to be a piece of bread.

SYNONYM: **pasada de** *adj.* *(Spain)* • (lit.): a passage of.

pesado/a *adj.* dull, tiresome, annoying, irritating, pain in the neck • (lit.): heavy, massive, weighty.

example: Darío es un **pesado**. Siempre está contando historias aburridas.

translation: Dario is such a **pain in the neck**. He is always telling boring stories.

SYNONYM -1: **cargante** *adj.* • (lit.): loaded.

SYNONYM -2: **latoso/a** *adj.*

NOTE: This comes from the expression *dar la lata,* (literally meaning "to give the tin can," is used to mean "to annoy the living daylights out of someone"). pleasant, funny • (lit.): amenable.

ANTONYM: **chunguero** *adj.*

NOTE: This comes from the term *chunga* meaning "joke" or "jest."

pez gordo *m.* person of great importance, "big wig" • (lit.): fat fish.

example: Algún día yo seré el **pez gordo** de esta compañía.

translation: Someday I'll be the **big cheese** in this company.

SYNONYM: **de peso** *adj.* • (lit.): of weight, weighty.

example: Ese señor es una persona **de peso**.

translation: That man's a **big wig**.

pila *f.* a bunch of, a lot of, a pile of • (lit.): sink, basin.

example: Estoy muy ocupado. Tengo una **pila** de cosas que hacer.

translation: I'm very busy. I have **a bunch of** things to do.

SYNONYM: **montón** *m.* • (lit.): crowd – *see p. 222*

pincharse una llanta *exp.* to get a flat tire • (lit.): to puncture a tire.

example: Ayer llegué tarde a la escuela porque se me **pinchó una llanta**.

translation: Yesterday I arrived late to school because I **got a flat tire**.

NOTE: There are many different terms for "tire" depending on the country:

SYNONYM -1: **caucho** *m.* *(Venezuela).*

SYNONYM -2: **cubierta** *f.* *(Argentina / Uruguay).*

SYNONYM -3: **goma** *f.* *(Argentina / Uruguay).*

SYNONYM -4: **llanta** *f.* *(Latin America).*

SYNONYM -5: **neumático** *m.* *(Spain).*

SYNONYM -6: **rueda** *f.* *(Spain).*

piropo *m.* compliment.

example: A Ana siempre le echan muchos **piropos** porque es una mujer muy bella.

translation: Ana always receives many **compliments** because she's a very beautiful woman.

NOTE: **echar un piropo** *exp.* to give a compliment.

pitillo *m.* cigarette • (lit.): small whistle.

example: Pedro tiene mal aliento porque siempre tiene un **pitillo** en la boca.

translation: Pedro has bad breath because he always has a **cigarette** hanging from his mouth.

SYNONYM -1: **faso** *m. (Argentina).*

SYNONYM -2: **pucho** *m. (Argentina)* • (lit.): cigarette butt.

plata *f.* money • (lit.): silver.

example: En los Estados Unidos los jugadores de baloncesto ganan mucha **plata**.

translation: In the U.S., basketball players make a lot of **money**.

SYNONYMS: SEE - **lana**, *p. 217.*

ALSO: **podrido/a de dinero (estar)** *exp.* to be rich • to be rolling in money • (lit.): to be rotten in money.

NOTE: Any synonym for *dinero* may be substituted.

platicar *v. (Mexico)* to have a little chat, to talk.

example: Me encanta **platicar** con Darío. ¡Es tan inteligente y simpático!

translation: I love to **talk** with Darío. He's so smart and nice!

SYNONYM -1: **charlar** *v. (Argentina / Spain / Uruguay / Cuba).*

SYNONYM -2: **dar la lata** *exp. (Puerto Rico / Cuba).*

poli *f.* a popular abbreviation for *policía* meaning "police," or "cops."

example: ¡Corre que viene la **poli**!

translation: Run! The **cops** are coming!

SYNONYM -1: **cana** *f. (Argentina).*

SYNONYM -2: **chota** *f.*

¿Qué hay de nuevo? *exp.* What's new? • (lit.): [same].

example: **¿Qué hay de nuevo** Sergio? ¡Hace tiempo que no te veo!

translation: **What's new**, Sergio? It's been a long time!

NOTE: **de nuevo** *adv.* again.

example: Lo hizo **de nuevo**.

translation: He / She did it again.

SYNONYM -1: **¿Qué hubo?** *exp.* • (lit.): What was? / What had?

SYNONYM -2: **¿Qué onda?** *exp.* • (lit.): What wave?

SYNONYM -3: **¿Qué haces, papá?** *exp. (Argentina)* What are you up to, pal? • (lit.): What are you doing, pops?

¡Qué va! *exclam.* Baloney! No way! Get out of here! • (lit.): What goes!

example: ¿Tú crees que va a llover hoy?
!Qué va! ¿No ves que hace sol?

translation: Do you think it's going to rain today?
No way! Don't you see the sun is out?

SYNONYM -1: **¡Qué bobada!** *exclam.* What nonsense!

SYNONYM -2: **¡Qué disparate!** *exclam.* What baloney!

SYNONYM -3: **¡Qué tontería!** *exclam.* What stupidity!

NOTE: This exclamation is not used in Argentina or Uruguay.

raro/a *adj.* weird, strange, peculiar • (lit.): rare.

example: Los Gonzalez son muy **raros**. Nunca salen de su casa.

translation: The Gonzalez's are very **weird**. They never leave their house.

ALSO: **rara vez** *exp.* seldom • (lit.): rare time.

SYNONYM: **lunático/a** *adj. & n.* • (lit.): lunatic.

rechulo/a *adj.* very "cool," neat.

example: Este libro está **rechulo**.

translation: This book is really **cool**.

NOTE: In Spanish, it is very popular to attach the prefix "re" to the beginning of an adjective for greater emphasis: *bonito* = beautiful • ***re****bonito* = really beautiful *fuerte* = strong • ***re****fuerte* = really strong, etc.

SYNONYM -1: **chévere** *adj.* *(Puerto Rico).*

SYNONYM -2: **¡Qué grande!** *interj. (Argentina).*

SYNONYM -3: **¡Qué Guay!** *interj. (Spain).*

regalito *m.* a lousy present or gift (usually used sarcastically) • (lit.): small gift.

example: ¡Vaya **regalito**! ¡Mi papá me dio un dólar de regalo de cumpleaños!

translation: What a **great gift**! My dad gave me one dollar for my birthday!

regatear *v. (a popular soccer term)* to hoard • (lit.): to bargain.

example: Los otros jugadores odian a Maradona porque le gusta **regatear** mucho.

translation: The other players can't stand Maradona because he likes to **hoard** the ball a lot.

NOTE: This refers to the act of hoarding the ball in a soccer game.

SYNONYM: **chupar** *v.* • (lit.): to suck.

renacuajo/a *n.* little kid, small child, shrimp, little runt • (lit.): tadpole.

example: En la casa de Manuel siempre hay un montón de **renacuajos**.

translation: There's always a lot of **small kids** at Manuel's house.

SYNONYM -1: **chiquillo/a** *n.*

NOTE: This noun comes from the adjective *chico/a* meaning "small."

SYNONYM -2: **chiquitín/a** *n.*

NOTE: This noun comes from the adjective *chico/a* meaning "small."

SYNONYM -3: **crío/a** *m.* • (lit.): a nursing-baby.

SYNONYM -4: **escuincle** *m.* little kid, small child.

SYNONYM -5: **gurrumino/a** *n.* • (lit.): weak or sickly person, "whimp."

SYNONYM -6: **mocoso/a** *n.* • (lit.): snotty-nosed person.

SYNONYM -7: **párvulo** *m.* • (lit.): tot.

SYNONYM -8: **pequeñajo/a** *n.*

NOTE: This noun comes from the adjective *pequeño/a* meaning "small."

SYNONYM -9: **pituso/a** *n.* smurf (from the cartoon characters).

ANTONYM -1: **grandote** *m.*

NOTE: This noun comes from the adjective *grande* meaning "big."

ANTONYM -2: **grandullón/a** *n.* big kid.

NOTE: This noun comes from the adjective *grande* meaning "big."

reventar *v.* • **1.** to annoy, to bug • **2.** to tire someone out • (lit.): to burst.

example (1): Me **revienta** cuando llegas tarde.

translation: It **bugs** me when you're late.

example (2): ¡Ernesto come tanto que un día de estos ¡va a **reventar**!

translation: Pedro eats so much that one of these days he's going to **explode**!

SYNONYM: **matar** *v. (Spain)* • (lit.): to kill.

reventón *m.* party • (lit.): bursting, explosion.

example: Esta noche vamos a ir a un **reventón**.

translation: Tonight we are going to a **party**.

SYNONYMS: SEE - **pachanga**, *p. 224*.

robot *m.* deadhead, person who doesn't show his / her feelings, apathetic person • (lit.): robot.

example: Julio es un **robot**. Nunca se rie.

translation: Julio is a **deadhead**. He never laughs.

rollo *m.* • **1.** ordeal • **2.** long boring speech or conversation • **3.** boring person or thing • **4.** *(Spain)* movie, film, story • (lit.): roll, paper roll.

example (1): ¡Qué **rollo**! ¡Ahora se me descompuso mi carro!

translation: What an **ordeal**! Now my car broke down!

example (2): El discuro de Augusto es tan **rollo** que me estoy quedando dormido.

translation: Augusto's speech is so **boring** I'm falling asleep.

example (3): Ese tipo es un **rollo**. Me estoy quedando dormido de escucharle hablar.

translation: That guy is so **boring**. I'm falling asleep just by listening to him talk.

example (4): Esta noche hay un buen **rollo** en la televisión.

translation: There's a good move on television tonight.

ALSO -1: **meter un rollo** *exp.* to lie, to tell a lie • (lit.): to introduce a roll.

ALSO -2: **¡Qué rollo!** *interj.* How boring!

ALSO -3: **soltar el rollo** *exp.* to talk a lot • (lit.): to set free or let go a roll.

romper a *v.* to burst out, to do something suddenly.

example: Parecía que Agustín iba a **romper a** reir cuando se enteró que ganó la lotería.

translation: It seemed like Agustin was going to **burst out** laughing when he found out he won the lottery.

SYNONYM -1: **echarse a** *v.* • (lit.): to throw oneself to • *echarse a llorar / reir;* to burst out crying / laughing.

SYNONYM -2: **largar** *v.* *(Argentina)* • (lit.): to release.

SYNONYM -3: **poner a** *v.* • (lit.): to put.

suertudo/a *adj.* lucky person.

example: Paco es un **suertudo**. Ya ha ganado la lotería dos veces.

translation: Paco is such a **lucky person**. He won the lottery twice already.

supercontento/a (estar) *adj.* ultra happy.

example: Ernesto está **super-contento** con su motocicleta nueva.

translation: Ernesto is **ultra happy** with his new motorcycle.

ALSO: **pegando saltos (estar)** *exp.* to be jumping for joy • (lit.): to be jumping.

talego *m.* jail, prison.

example: ¡Si sigues portándote así vas a acabar en el **talego**!

translation: If you continue to behave that way, you're going to end up in **jail**!

SYNONYM -1: **bote** *m.* • (lit.): rowboat.

SYNONYM -2: **cana** *f. (Argentina)* • **1.** prison, "slammer" • **2.** police (as seen earlier).

SYNONYM -3: **fondo** *m. (Puerto Rico)* • (lit.): the bottom.

NOTE: **acabar en el talego / bote** *exp.* to end up in jail, in the "slammer."

tertulia *f.* social gathering, "get-together."

example: Todos los sábados por la noche tenemos una **tertulia** en casa de Ramón.

translation: Every Saturday night, we have a **get-together** at Ramon's house.

ALSO: **tertulia (estar de)** *exp.* to talk, to chat.

SYNONYM -1: **charla** *f.* (from the verb *charlar* meaning "to chat").

SYNONYM -2: **movida** *f. (Spain).*

testarudo *adj.* stubborn, headstrong.

example: Javier es un **testarudo**. Cuando se le mete una idea en la cabeza, nunca cambia de opinión.

translation: Javier is so **stubborn**. When he gets an idea in his head, he never changes his mind.

NOTE: This comes from the feminine latin word *testa* meaning "head."

SYNONYM -1: **cabezón** *adj.* • **1.** headstrong • **2.** big-headed.

NOTE: This term comes from the feminine noun *cabeza* meaning "head."

SYNONYM -2: **machacón** *adj.* • (lit.): boring, tiresome.

SYNONYM -3: **terco** *adj.* • (lit.): obstinate, stubborn.

SYNONYM -4: **tozudo** *adj.* • (lit.): obstinate, stubborn.

tía *f. (Spain / Cuba)* girl, "chick" • (lit.): type.

example: ¡Mira esa **tipa**! ¡Me gusta su minifalda!

translation: Look at that **chick**! I like her miniskirt!

SYNONYM -1: **mina** *f. (Argentina)*

SYNONYM -2: **tipa** *f.* • (lit.): aunt.

ANTONYM -1: **tío** *m. (Cuba / Spain)* guy, "dude" • (lit.): uncle.

ANTONYM -2: **tipo** *m.* • (lit.): type.

tío *m. (Cuba / Spain)* guy, "dude" • (lit.): uncle.

example: Conozco a ese **tío**. Solía ir a mi escuela.

translation: I know that **guy**. He used to go to my school.

NOTE: **tía** *f.* girl, "chick" • (lit.): aunt.

SYNONYM: **tipo** *m. (Mexico / Puerto Rico / Argentina)* guy, "dude" • (lit.): type.

ALSO: **tipa** *f.* girl, "chick" • (lit.): type.

tipo *m.* guy, "dude" • (lit.): type.

example: ¡Ese **tipo** está loco!

translation: That **guy** is crazy!

SYNONYM: **tío** *m. (Spain)* • (lit.): uncle.

ANTONYM: **tipa** *f.* girl, "chick."

tragar *v.* • **1.** to eat • **2.** to drink • (lit.): to swallow.

example: ¿Tienes hambre? ¿Quieres algo de **tragar**?

translation: Are you hungry? Do you want something to **eat**?

SYNONYM -1: **embuchar** *v.* to eat • (lit.): to cram food into the beak of a bird.

SYNONYM -2: **jalar** *v. (Spain).*

SYNONYM -3: **jamar** *v.*

SYNONYM -4: **morfar** *v. (Argentina).*

SYNONYM -5: **papear** *v. (Spain).*

SYNONYM -6: **zampar** *v.* • (lit.): to stuff or cram (food) down, to gobble down.

trapos *m.* clothes • (lit.): rags.

example: Manuela tiene unos **trapos** muy bonitos.

translation: Manuela has very nice **clothes**.

SYNONYM -1: **paños** *m.* • (lit.): rags.

SYNONYM -2: **pilchas** *f.pl.* *(Argentina)*.

SYNONYM -3: **ropaje** *m.* • (lit.): robes.

ALSO -1: **poner a uno como un trapo** *exp.* to give someone a severe reprimand • (lit.): to put oneself like an old rug.

ALSO -2: **sacar los trapos a relucir** *exp.* to air one's dirty laundry in public • (lit.): to take one's dirty laundry to shine.

trastornado/a (estar) *adj.* to be furious, angry.

example: El jefe está **trastornado** porque Pepe no terminó el trabajo.

translation: The boss is **furious** because Pepe didn't finish his job.

SYNONYM -1: **cabreado/a** *adj.* (to be) all worked up (over something).

ALSO: **agarrar / pillar un cabreo** *exp.* to fly off the handle.

SYNONYM -2: **pusarse loco/a** *exp.* *(Puerto Rico)* to cause to go crazy (with anger).

SYNONYM -3: **rabioso/a** *adj.* • (lit.): rabid (or full of rabies).

tratar(se) + de *exp.* to be about, to pertain to • (lit.): to treat oneself of.

example (1): Esta obra de teatro **trata de** Don Quijote.

translation: This play **is about** Don Quixote.

example (2): ¿De qué **se trata**?

translation: What **is this about**?

tropezar con alguien *exp.* to run into someone, to bump into someone • (lit.): to trip or stumble with someone.

example: Ayer **tropecé con** Antonio Rodriquez y lo encontré muy delgado.

translation: Yesterday I **bumped into** Antonio Rodriquez and he looked really thin to me.

SYNONYM -1: **chocarme con alguien** *exp.* *(Argentina)* • (lit.): to collide oneself with someone.

SYNONYM -2: **toparse con alguien** *exp.* *(Spain / Puerto Rico / Cuba)* • (lit.): to bump oneself with someone.

trupe *f.* group of friends or family members, (the whole) gang.

example: Me encanta ir de vacaciones con toda la **trupe**.

translation: I love going on vacation with the whole **gang**.

SYNONYM -1: **ganga** *f.* *(Puerto Rico)* applies to a whole family or group of friends.

SYNONYM -2: **peña** *f.* *(Spain)*.

vacilar *v.* • **1.** to joke around, to clown around, to tease • **2.** to have a good time • **3.** to show off.

example (1): A Manuel le gusta **vacilar**.

translation: Manuel loves to **joke around**.

example (2): Me encanta **vacilar** con mis amigos los sábados por la noche.

translation: I love **having a good time** with my friends on Saturday nights.

example (3): Me gusta mucho **vacilar** con mi moto nueva.

translation: I love **showing off** my new motorcycle.

ALSO: **vacilón** *m.* • **1.** spree, party, shindig • **2.** something funny, cool, neat.

SYNONYM -1: **bromar** *v. (Spain)* (from the feminine noun *broma* meaning "joke").

SYNONYM -2: **chirigotear** *v.* to clown around.

SYNONYM -3: **pitorrearse** *v.* • **1.** to clown around • **2.** to make fun of someone.

vale *interj.* okay, "you got a deal" • (lit.): worth.

example: ¿Quieres ir al cine conmigo?
¡**Vale**!

translation: Do you want to go to the movies with me?
Okay!

NOTE: This interjection comes from the verb *valer* meaning "to have worth."

ALSO: ¡**Sí vale**! *interj.* Why, yes!

SYNONYM -1: **genial** *adj. (Argentina).*

SYNONYM -2: **OK** *interj.*

NOTE: This interjection has been borrowed from English and is becoming increasingly popular throughout the Spanish-speaking countries.

¡Vaya! *interj.* • **1.** *(used to indicate surprise or amazement)* Well! How about that! • **2.** *(commonly used to modify a noun)* What an amazing... • **3.** *(used to modify a statement)* Really! • (lit.): Go!

example (1): ¡**Vaya**! Parece que va a empezar a llover.

translation: **How about that**! It looks like it's going to start raining.

example (2): ¡**Vaya** equipo! • !**Vaya** calor!

translation: **What a** team! • **What** heat!

example (3): Es un buen tipo, ¡**vaya**!

translation: What a good guy. **Really**!

SYNONYM -1: **¡Che!** *interj. (Argentina).*

SYNONYM -2: **¡Vamos!** *interj.* • (lit.): Let's go!

NOTE -1: *Vamos* may also be used within a sentence to indicate that the speaker has just changed his/her mind or is making a clarification. In this case, *vamos* is translated as "well."

example: Es guapa. **Vamos**, no es fea.

translation: She's pretty. **Well**, she's not ugly.

NOTE -2: Both *vaya* and *vamos* are extremely popular and both come from the verb *ir* meaning "to go."

verse con alguien *exp.* to meet someone • (lit.): to see oneself with someone.

example: Mañana me voy a **ver con** mi jefe. Espero que me aumente el sueldo.

translation: Tomorrow I'm going to **meet with** my boss. I hope he's going to raise my salary.

ALSO: **quedar con alguien** *exp.* to make an appointment with someone • (lit.): to remain with someone.

viejos *m.pl.* parents, folks • (lit.): the old ones.

example: Me encanta ir a casa de mis **viejos** porque siempre hay algo bueno de comer.

translation: I love going to my **folks** because there is always something good to eat.

NOTE -1: **viejo** *m.* • **1.** father • **2.** husband • (lit.): old man.

NOTE -2: **vieja** *f.* • **1.** mother • **2.** wife • (lit.): old woman.

vivo *adj. (Argentina, Uruguay, Spain)* smart, clever, bright • (lit.): alive.

example: Alvaro es un **vivo**. Siempre se sale con la suya.

translation: Alvaro is so **smart**. Everything always goes his way.

SYNONYM -1: **despabilado/a** *adj.*

SYNONYM -2: **despierto/a** *adj.* • (lit.): awaken.

SYNONYM -3: **espabilado/a** *adj. (Spain).*

SYNONYM -4: **listillo/a** *adj.*

NOTE: This comes from the adjective *listo* meaning "clear" or "smart."

SYNONYM -5: **pillo** *adj.* • (lit.): roguish, mischievous.

ANTONYM -1: **adoquín** *adj.* • (lit.): paving block.

ANTONYM -2: **bruto/a** *adj.* • (lit.): stupid, crude.

ANTONYM -3: **cabezota** *adj.* • (lit.): big-headed.

NOTE: This comes from the feminine noun *cabeza* meaning "head."

ANTONYM -4: **tosco/a** *adj.* • (lit.): coarse, crude, unrefined.

ANTONYM -5: **zopenco/a** *adj.* • (lit.): dull, stupid.

ORDER FORM

P.O. Box 519 • Fulton, CA 95439 • USA

TOLL FREE Telephone/FAX (US/Canada):
1-888-4-ESLBOOKS (1-888-437-5266)

International orders Telephone/FAX line:
707-546-8878

Name ______________________________

(School/Company) ______________________________

Street Address ______________________________

City ______________ State/Province ______________ Postal Code ______________

Country ______________ Phone ______________

Quantity	Title	Book or Cassette?	Price Each	Total Price

Total for Merchandise	
Sales Tax (California Residents Only)	
Shipping (See Below)	
ORDER TOTAL	

METHOD OF PAYMENT (check one)

☐ Check or Money Order ☐ VISA ☐ Master Card ☐ American Express ☐ Discover

(Money orders and personal checks must be in U.S. funds and drawn on a U.S. bank.)

Credit Card Number: ☐☐☐☐☐☐☐☐☐☐☐☐☐☐☐☐ Card Expires: ☐☐ ☐☐

Signature *(important!)* ➔

SHIPPING

Domestic Orders: SURFACE MAIL (delivery time 5-7 days).
Add $4 shipping/handling for the first item · $1 for each additional item.
RUSH SERVICE available at extra charge.

International Orders: OVERSEAS SURFACE (delivery time 6-8 weeks).
Add $5 shipping/handling for the first item · $2 for each additional item.
OVERSEAS AIRMAIL available at extra charge.